MW01519871

Cottage Radio
&
Other Plays

Dear Vlad,

Thank you so much
for being the original
Gordon!

lots of
love,
[signature]

Cottage Radio

& Other Plays

COTTAGE RADIO, WHITE WEDDING & POST ALICE

TAYLOR MARIE GRAHAM

TALONBOOKS

Talonbooks
9259 Shaughnessy Street, Vancouver, British Columbia, Canada V6P 6R4
talonbooks.com

Talonbooks is located on xʷməθkʷəy̓əm, Sḵwx̱wú7mesh, and səlilwətaɫ Lands.

First printing: 2024

Typeset in Minion
Printed and bound in Canada on 100% post-consumer recycled paper

Cover photograph by Muhammed Öçal via unsplash.com
Inside cover photograph by Lukas Pereira via pexels.com

Talonbooks acknowledges the financial support of the Canada Council for the Arts, the Government of Canada through the Canada Book Fund, and the Province of British Columbia through the British Columbia Arts Council and the Book Publishing Tax Credit.

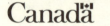  

Rights to produce *Cottage Radio & Other Plays*, in whole or in part, in any medium by any group, amateur or professional, are retained by the author. Interested persons are requested to contact Talonbooks at info@talonbooks.com.

Library and Archives Canada Cataloguing in Publication

Title: Cottage radio & other plays : Cottage radio, White wedding, & Post Alice / Taylor Marie Graham.
Other titles: Cottage radio and other plays
Names: Graham, Taylor Marie, author. | Container of (work): Graham, Taylor Marie. Cottage radio. | Container of (work): Graham, Taylor Marie. White wedding. | Container of (work): Graham, Taylor Marie. Post Alice.
Identifiers: Canadiana 20240321375 | ISBN 9781772016185 (softcover)
Subjects: LCGFT: Drama.
Classification: LCC PS8613.R3475 C68 2024 | DDC C812/.6—dc23

To all complex rural women out there who inspire me each and every old day

PLAYWRIGHT'S INTRODUCTION

Well, hello. This is certainly a treat.

I honestly can't believe that I'm here, introducing you to a book (a whole book!) full of plays by little old me. You are about to meet three works of theatre that I've put out in the world over the last decade – *Cottage Radio, White Wedding,* and *Post Alice.*

These three plays chart a chronological history of my career as a playwright to date. First you'll find *Cottage Radio,* which is my MFA in creative writing thesis project developed at the University of Guelph in 2014. This three-act dramedy with original music is inspired by the F3 tornado which hit Goderich, Ontario, in 2011. Next you'll find *White Wedding* from 2017, which is a one-act site-specific comedy, set on the outskirts of a rural wedding reception. The final play, *Post Alice,* premiered in 2021. It is deeply inspired by Alice Munro's writing and one of Ontario's most mysterious missing persons cases from the last thirty years.

While I've been working with my exceedingly patient editor, getting these plays ready to sit side-by-side as you'll find them here, I've been thinking a lot about what they might mean together. I've been wondering about how they might connect or collide, about what they might have to say to the world (if that's what plays are supposed to do), and what you as the reader might get out of spending some time with them all in a row. I don't know if I have these completely figured out exactly, but they all undeniably share at least one element in common: they are set in my home region of Huron County, Ontario.

When I think of my childhood home, I imagine the Lake Huron shoreline. I see stones and sand meeting the water, which expands sea-like in a seemingly endless reach of blue to the other side. My imagination also takes me deeper to a cavern of white far below the surface, where the world's largest salt mine sits under the waves. On land heading east, I see soybean and hay fields. I follow cars along country roads to abandoned airport runways in Port Albert, to Alice Munro's old farmhouse outside Wingham, to theatre stages in Blyth, to high school gymnasiums in Clinton, to stagecoach ghosts in Exeter, to late-night beach parties in Grand Bend, to the pretty shops of Bayfield, to the delicious cream puffs in Goderich, and everywhere else around, through, and in between.

I think of all the stories I know from my childhood layered on top of the land. These stories' heroes are often the hilarious Huron County women from my youth. In my mind, I watch as they work hard to keep our lives full of all the necessities, like fresh corn on the cob, loud music to sing into, campfire stories full of brave truth, and the kind of laughter that lives in your belly for years. I think of all the Huron Tract stories from this land that I don't know, too. I wonder about those stories I can't see that came before me and will come after me. I wonder at their shapes and structures, embedded throughout the shallow hills and farms and small-town main streets of the region.

When I look at these plays today, I see the questions I was obsessed with at the time. For *Cottage Radio*: What is home? What happens when your home is destroyed? How do families come together through tragedy? What forces the truth to surface and what does it mean to rebuild? When I wrote *White Wedding*, I was wondering what would happen if I tried writing a festival-style comedy. I wanted to see if I could write a piece that explored those less public moments at a wedding, the ones nobody sees. Questions of nostalgia and old friendships crept their way in, too, as they always do for me. You'll find these questions in *Post Alice* too, as well as possible answers to other questions rolling around in my brain such as: What's life like in Alice Munro Country? What really happened to Mistie Murray, who disappeared from Goderich in 1995? How do we face our most terrifying wounds? What does it mean to be treaty people? Where do our lost girls go?

The three plays strive to tell you a little something about my version of Huron County, which, of course, is different from other people's versions. These plays try to show you some sense of the people and places I think of as my home. For me, as you'll see, this home is a complex place full of the beautiful contradictions that make up a life. Noteworthy sunsets meet rotating thunderstorms, family bonds meet missing women, star-filled skies meet pangs of nostalgia, settler ambiguity meets blood-soaked fingers, and highly charged adventures eventually meet the cliff's edge.

Do me a favour and spend some time with the names of the many incredible folks I thank in my acknowledgements at the back of this book. As a team sport, theatre truly takes many talented people to get it off the ground. It's because of each and every one of them that these plays and this book even exist at all. I am so grateful for the amazing artists I've had the opportunity to work with along the way.

And thanks to you too, dear reader. It's an honour and a privilege to guide you along my favourite Southwestern Ontario shoreline. See you on the other side.

—TAYLOR MARIE GRAHAM

Cottage Radio

Top, left to right: Dave Martin, Jean-Phillipe Allanby, Madeline Leon, and Amanda Pereira in Alumnae Theatre's production of *Cottage Radio* at the Fireworks Festival, November 2015

Bottom, left to right: Amanda Pereira and Madeline Leon in Alumnae Theatre's production of *Cottage Radio* at the Fireworks Festival, November 2015

Photographs by Bruce Peters

PRODUCTION HISTORY

Cottage Radio was developed as Taylor Marie Graham's MFA in Creative Writing thesis project at the University of Guelph and first produced from August 19 to 31, 2014, at The Livery Theatre in Goderich, Ontario, with the following cast and crew:

CHRISTINA:	Lara Mrkoci
NADINE:	Tiana Asperjan
JASPER:	Joshua Browne
GORDON:	Vladimir Jon Cubrt
SUSAN:	Lindy Linfield

Director:	Jill Harper
Musical Arranger:	Jonas Bonnetta
Set Designer:	Christine Groom
Sound Designer:	Steph Berntson
Lighting Designer:	Simon Rossiter
Stage Manager:	Lynette Blanchard

CHARACTERS

CHRISTINA: In her early thirties, Nadine's older sister, Susan's granddaughter, Gordon's daughter, Jasper's childhood best friend and ex-girlfriend, drummer in the band Cottage Radio, host of the radio show *Cottage Radio*. Also known as Chris. Very funny and sarcastic, to deflect. Deeply sensitive and cares fiercely about people she loves. Stuck. Hurt. Sharp. Alcoholic. Lonely. Angry. Desperate for love.

NADINE: In her late twenties, Christina's younger sister, Susan's granddaughter, Gordon's daughter, guitar and vocals in the band Cottage Radio. Moved away to Toronto. Organized. Funny. Ambitious. Very musically talented. Wants to help others. Healing but lonely. Homesick but cautious.

JASPER: Same age as Christina, not blood-related to the rest of the characters, has always been in love with Christina, second guitar and vocals in the band Cottage Radio. A little oblivious to the consequences of his actions. Idealizes people and places. Very charming. Adventurous. Sensitive. A good heart.

GORDON: In his mid-fifties, Christina and Nadine's father and Susan's son-in-law. Overindulges with alcohol, silence, and solitude. Heartbroken through and through. Former competitive rower.

SUSAN: In her late seventies or early eighties, Christina and Nadine's grandmother, and Gordon's mother-in-law. Strong. Funny. Independent. A caretaker. Wants to help her family heal and move on.

SAM: (*played by the actor playing JASPER*) Caller, fan of *Cottage Radio*.

JOANNE: (*played by the actor playing NADINE*) Caller, shocked mother, tornado victim.

MARCUS: (*played by the actor playing JASPER*) Caller, angry, tornado victim.

LAURIE ANNE: (*played by the actor playing SUSAN*) Caller, chatty, married to Frank, tornado victim.

TOM: (*played by the actor playing GORDON*) Caller, good storyteller, tornado victim.

JANE: (*played by the actor playing SUSAN*) Caller, avid walker, tornado victim.

LEO: (*played by the actor playing JASPER*) Caller, works for the radio station.

RALPH: (*played by the actor playing JASPER*) Caller, married to Rhonda, tornado victim.

RHONDA: (*played by the actor playing NADINE*) Caller, married to Ralph, tornado victim.

SETTING

An old family cottage just outside Goderich, Ontario, on Lake Huron. The cottage is littered with memorabilia of decades past: awards and old achievements on the walls, boating equipment, old comfortable furniture that has been sent here to slowly die, and mismatched attempts at making the space look decade-appropriate clash together all around. The audience sees an open living space with doors leading to bedrooms and the bathroom and the kitchen. There is an area set up as a makeshift radio station. A deck outside leads to the beach.

Realistic or impressionist reimaginings of this set are both very welcome. Basic realistic props are encouraged. Feel free to get creative with where and how the callers come into the space.

TIME

The Goderich tornado hit Huron County, Ontario, on August 21, 2011.

MUSIC

Anyone interested in the music for the songs included in this play should contact the playwright.

Act 1

ACT 1, SCENE 1
LISTEN ALL THE TIME

Mid-morning. GORDON is asleep on the floor. CHRISTINA is asleep on the couch. There is a mess of chip bags and beers left from the night before. SUSAN enters carrying bags of groceries and a couple of metal animals made for the garden. She sees the mess and starts cleaning and putting groceries away. She puts together bowls of cereal and milk and puts them on the coffee table. SUSAN exits to the bedroom. Some time passes. SUSAN enters from the bedroom in her bathing suit, holding a towel. She grabs a Goderich Signal Star *newspaper from her grocery bag and a nearby alarm clock. She places the alarm clock and the newspaper near CHRISTINA's head. SUSAN looks over at GORDON, sighs, and walks over to the wall, where she pulls down an old rowing medal of his and puts it in his hand. She also grabs a rowing magazine and puts it out for him. SUSAN exits to the beach. The alarm clock rings. GORDON wakes up. He is very hungover; he takes a moment to recognize the medal in his hand. He gets up and struggles to walk over to turn off the alarm clock. Just as he is about to turn it off, CHRISTINA reaches out and turns it off.*

GORDON: You jerk.

CHRISTINA laughs.

CHRISTINA: What? Were you gonna get that?

GORDON: Well, that's it then.

CHRISTINA: What?

GORDON: You made me do this.

GORDON straightens out his body.

CHRISTINA: Wait. What? No. Don't!

GORDON: Timber!

GORDON falls towards CHRISTINA like a tree.

CHRISTINA: Dad. Dad! Get off! Jesus.

GORDON: Why? Is the tree hurting you?

CHRISTINA: No. You're just –

GORDON: Then why would the tree get off you?

CHRISTINA: Dad, you're –

GORDON: What is the tree doing?

CHRISTINA: Hurting. Me. The tree is hurting me. I am hurt
by the tree!

GORDON: That's what I thought. And you're?

CHRISTINA: Sorry. I'm sorry. I'm sorry, Mr. Tree, but
you're hurting me!

GORDON: Okay.

GORDON gets up.

CHRISTINA: Good morning.

GORDON: Morning.

GORDON grabs a bowl of cereal and the newspaper.

CHRISTINA: Oh, Dad. The newspaper.

GORDON: The newspaper. Made by trees.

CHRISTINA: I need it. For work.

GORDON: Oh, yeah.

> *GORDON hands back the newspaper. He walks over to the fridge and pulls out three beers.*

CHRISTINA: I thought you might listen today.

GORDON: I always listen.

CHRISTINA: Yeah, but I mean –

GORDON: I listen all the time.

> *GORDON gives CHRISTINA a beer. GORDON exits to the deck with beers and cereal.*
>
> *CHRISTINA begins to set up her radio broadcast. She opens up the newspaper and circles some things. She eats some of the cereal. A flashing light counts down three, two, one.*

CHRISTINA: And welcome back to the *Cottage Radio* program, your midday radio snack from beach country, Huron County. Yes, my Goderich friends, this would be your old pal Chris Marley working you through another sticky August afternoon from the comfort of my grandmother's cottage living room. Hello, Goderich.

First on the block for notices, it looks like there was a Timbits soccer tournament that started at GDCI this morning at 9 a.m. I have a feeling there may still be some kiddies running around after a ball in a field looking sweaty and cute as ever right now, so if you have any updates about this monumental moment in sports history, give me a call and I may just let you give us a play-by-play over the radio. Who knows, this may just be your baby girl's fifteen minutes of fame. We want to hear all about it, don't we Goderich?

*SUSAN enters from the beach onto the deck. She gives
GORDON a rock from the beach.*

CHRISTINA: And next up is the flea market. Every Sunday like
today through the summer, my friends, but you already knew
that. She'll be out until 3 p.m. Get yourself some old stuff, which
then will become your sexy new stuff, I suppose.

SUSAN enters the cottage.

CHRISTINA: And there she is. I have a feeling, Goderich, if we
are lucky, Susan Marley, just in from the water, was at the flea
market this very morning. And if we're super lucky, we might
even be able to find what beauty product she got a hold of for us
today – oh, and there we are. Two pigs.

SUSAN: (*into the microphone*) Two frogs.

CHRISTINA: Two frogs. Frogs. My mistake, Goderich. Two
little metal frogs on metal spikes. For the garden, I'm
assuming, Grandma?

SUSAN: Over where Gordon is sitting.

CHRISTINA: Wow. These two little metal frogs are sure going
to make that spot over there at the edge of our deck look
spectacular. Well done, Grandma. You really do find the nicest
junk of all.

SUSAN: Somebody made that junk, Christina.

CHRISTINA: And you bought it. I'm sure they thank you for that!

SUSAN: Well, maybe if you came to town with me some time, you
could pick out whatever junk you'd prefer.

CHRISTINA: Grandma, I –

SUSAN: That's what I like, so that's what I buy.

CHRISTINA: I know, I was just –

SUSAN: If you want different junk, all you have to do is get out of this living room and come with me and get it. But you won't do that, will you?

CHRISTINA: Grandma –

SUSAN: You won't even accompany your dear old grandma into town.

CHRISTINA: For a lady who just went for a relaxing dip in the lake, you sure are easy to get going.

A red light flashes. SAM enters.

SUSAN: Isn't that a caller?

CHRISTINA: Right you are, Grandma.

CHRISTINA hits a button.

CHRISTINA: Hello, *Cottage Radio.*

SAM: Hello?

CHRISTINA: Would this be a Timbits soccer tournament update?

SAM: Uh – no.

CHRISTINA: Are you about to give us a live broadcast from the flea market?

SAM: Nope.

CHRISTINA: Well then, you must be calling to let us know about the christening going on over at St. Peter's this aft., which I haven't even been able to get to yet today.

SAM: That wasn't the plan.

SUSAN: Oh, why don't you let the man get on with it?

CHRISTINA: Sorry caller, but it appears my grandmother would like you to explain the reason as to why you called if you are not at the three hottest events of the season this afternoon.

SAM: I'm – well – is that really Chris Marley?

CHRISTINA: Yeah – why?

SAM: Oh my god. I just – *the* Chris Marley from the band Cottage Radio?

CHRISTINA: Oh, shit.

SUSAN: Christina, your language.

CHRISTINA: No caller, it's not.

SUSAN: Christina.

SAM: It's not?

CHRISTINA: Nope, it's not.

SAM: Oh.

SUSAN: It is!

CHRISTINA: Grandma.

SUSAN: The bright beautiful girl herself can be a bit –

CHRISTINA: What?

SUSAN: Can be a bit weird at times, but it is her.

CHRISTINA: Weird?

SUSAN: Go on. Tell him.

CHRISTINA: I really don't think –

SUSAN: Oh, don't listen to her. It is her, caller.

SAM: Really?

CHRISTINA: The one and only.

SAM: Awesome. Hi, Chris.

CHRISTINA: Hello, you.

SAM: I was just driving through Goderich today with my family and I flipped the channels on the radio and there you are! Chris Marley, so cool. The real Goderich experience. I've never even heard of this radio station.

CHRISTINA: That's kind of the point.

SUSAN: Christina.

SAM: Man, you guys were so right about this place, though. Goderich.

CHRISTINA: Were we?

SAM: Oh yeah. It really is the prettiest town in Canada.

CHRISTINA: Eh.

SUSAN: It's a beaut.

> *GORDON enters and walks across the room. He is visibly drunk.*

CHRISTINA: Well, it was the Queen that said it a while ago, not us. So thank her instead.

SAM: Okay.

CHRISTINA: It's on all those signs downtown, so you can see it there, I'm sure. You are downtown, aren't you?

SAM: Yeah. I, uh –

CHRISTINA: So can you see it on the signs? It is still on the signs, isn't it?

SAM: I, um –

SUSAN: Christina, why do you always have to –

GORDON hands CHRISTINA a record.

CHRISTINA: What are you doing, Dad?

SUSAN: Well, your caller wants to hear the song obviously.

CHRISTINA: Oh.

SAM: Yeah! Cool! Play it!

GORDON: Always, always listening.

CHRISTINA puts on the record.

ACT 1, SCENE 2
GODERICH SONG

In the past. JASPER, CHRISTINA, and NADINE play
"Goderich Song."

JASPER, CHRISTINA, and NADINE:
(*singing*) It sits standing up
On Huron the lake
Fish jumping up
The river right through
People go and say
Ontario don't shine
I say our town
Was built for you.

The town Bayfield up the road
Claims the prettiest sunsets
But my eyes don't lie
My feet getting wet
The piper bringin' in the day
With the sun
I'd take livin' in Goderich
Over anyone.

It's really just the same
As anywhere else
With a lake and a river
And a big courthouse
They hung poor jerks
In the jail way back
And the Queen hollered
"The prettiest town in Canada."

The lawyers shuffle round
The octagonal Square
Papers in their hand
And feet in the air

The drivers in their cars
Doing ringers round the Square
I'd take livin' in Goderich
Over anywhere.

JASPER, CHRISTINA, and NADINE sing the chorus ("It's really just the same …") twice more.

JASPER: I really think we should add a verse about Tiger Dunlop.

CHRISTINA: That guy with the red beard?

JASPER: The founder of Goderich.

NADINE: Oh yeah!

JASPER: Am I right, kiddo?

NADINE: Why is he not in our song already?

JASPER: Exactly. He needs to be in this song. I've been thinking about it for a while now.

NADINE: You're right. You're so right.

JASPER: I am right, kiddo. I am.

CHRISTINA: I – I don't know.

JASPER: What don't you know?

CHRISTINA: Isn't it – well, it's boring.

JASPER: Really?

NADINE: No.

CHRISTINA: It's boring.

NADINE: Well – just a little boring, maybe.

JASPER: But he, he fought tigers.

NADINE: That's not boring.

CHRISTINA: He didn't, though.

JASPER: He did!

CHRISTINA: There's no way that Scottish dude fought tigers. Not with that red beard. They would see him a mile away.

JASPER: In India the guy fought tigers. That's where he got his nickname, Tiger Dunlop. His real name was William or something.

CHRISTINA: Look, that's just what he wanted you to believe. Nobody actually fights tigers.

JASPER: Okay. But he did.

NADINE: If he did fight tigers, it would be cool to have him in our song.

CHRISTINA: But he didn't.

JASPER: Well, he was a super alcoholic.

NADINE: Oh yeah!

CHRISTINA: So?

JASPER: So, he had his help cart around bottles of whisky with him wherever he went. Barrels of it.

CHRISTINA: Allegedly.

NADINE: There are a lot of stories with this guy.

CHRISTINA: Exactly, stories. He may have been a good storyteller. But that's it.

JASPER: You're so wrong.

CHRISTINA: Besides, our mom and dad would get people to cart around whisky barrels behind them if they could afford it. What does that prove?

JASPER: Well, maybe your mom and dad need to fight tigers to become famous enough for people to cart around whisky bottles behind them, I don't know.

NADINE: Guys.

CHRISTINA: Look, there's just no way I'm letting that scary man into our song.

JASPER: What is so scary about Tiger Dunlop?

CHRISTINA: He's just –

NADINE: It's the beard. Chris is scared of his beard.

JASPER: No! That's so stupid.

NADINE: Dad used to have a beard. Terrified.

JASPER: Wow. Chris, that's hilarious.

CHRISTINA: It's not funny.

NADINE: It's pretty funny.

JASPER: Okay look. Everyone had beards back then. He was supposed to be a really funny guy, too, I think.

CHRISTINA: He's not going in the song.

JASPER: Well. He founded the goddamn town, we should put him in here more than the Queen, right kiddo?

NADINE: I – well, I –

JASPER: The Queen, she just commented one day that she thought it looked nice. Tiger spent years putting this place together, founding it.

CHRISTINA: Look, if you love the guy so much, maybe you should write a song all about him.

JASPER: Maybe I will.

CHRISTINA: But I am never playing it.

JASPER: It won't require drums.

CHRISTINA: Every good song requires drums.

JASPER: This one won't.

NADINE: Guys, can we just –

JASPER: I got it! One sec.

CHRISTINA: Oh you do, do ya? What have you got?

JASPER: Yup. It's all coming to me.

CHRISTINA: Jesus Christ.

NADINE: Jasper, you don't have to do this right now, I mean –

JASPER: Wait for it.

CHRISTINA: Oh I'm a waitin'.

NADINE: Jasper, really. Nobody is expecting you to –

JASPER: Here we go:
(*singing*) Tiger drank a lot of whisky
And had a beard all red
A twinkle in his eye
And ideas in his head.
He arrived on the land with Galt and said
"Hey ho, look at that! Goderich is its name and that's a fact!"

CHRISTINA and NADINE laugh really hard.

CHRISTINA: That's horrible.

JASPER: Hey!

NADINE: No, it's not horrible.

JASPER: You guys are not helping to form a safe creative space here.

CHRISTINA: Creative? You call that creative?

JASPER: Ow.

NADINE: No, no, no. Stop, Chris. What is it again, Jasper?

CHRISTINA: Yes. Please tell us again.

JASPER: I will tell you again.

NADINE: It started in C, right?

JASPER: Exactly, kiddo. (*singing*) Tiger drank a lot of whisky.

CHRISTINA: Guys, come on.

JASPER and NADINE:
(*singing*) And had a beard all red.

CHRISTINA: I'm so out of here.

JASPER and **NADINE:**
(*singing*) A twinkle in his eye
And ideas in his head.

CHRISTINA: I may never come back!

CHRISTINA exits.

JASPER and **NADINE:**
(*singing*) He arrived on the land with Galt and said,
"Hey ho, look at that!
Goderich is its name and that's a fact!"

It's really just the same
As anywhere else
With a lake and a river
And a big courthouse
They hung poor jerks
In the jail way back
And the Queen hollered
"The prettiest town in Canada!"

ACT 1, SCENE 3
THE CLOUDS

Present day in the cottage. Action continued from Scene 1. CHRISTINA, SUSAN, and GORDON are listening to the music, caught in their own pasts until the song ends.

CHRISTINA: Well, there you have it, dear caller. That was "Goderich Song" by none other than Cottage Radio. May we rest in peace. I hope that satisfied whatever rash you were looking to scratch there, and now for making the rest of us sit through that crap, I'm going to reward you with the best commercials Huron County has to offer. And go!

CHRISTINA pushes a button.

SUSAN: I think I prefer the version where your mom does backing vocals. Don't you, Gordon?

GORDON goes for another beer and takes it out to the deck.

SUSAN: I should really get him into the house for the night. He has that couple coming to see the place later today.

GORDON looks up at the sky.

CHRISTINA: Today? I think you'd have better luck getting trees to live in the house today. Look at him.

SUSAN: Well, somebody should live in that house if you two won't.

CHRISTINA: Who would want to live there when we have out here?

SUSAN looks at the sky.

SUSAN: Oh. Look at those clouds. Christina, take a look at this.

CHRISTINA jokes by turning around in the opposite direction and then grabs the newspaper and circles a few more things. SUSAN looks at CHRISTINA.

SUSAN: And you won't come in with me to show the place?

CHRISTINA laughs.

CHRISTINA: Grandma. The radio. I can't just leave.

SUSAN: Haven't made it all the way through the paper yet today?

CHRISTINA: Well, you know the *Goderich Signal Star*: dense. I don't think anybody can make it all the way through this bad boy.

SUSAN: So you haven't made it to page ten, then?

SUSAN starts to get ready to leave.

CHRISTINA: The marriages and engagements and all that? No. You know I don't go through all of those. If I did, that would be my whole broadcast some days and then I might miss somebody and then they'd really go berserk on me.

SUSAN: Gordon, we need to go into town. That couple'll be at the house soon.

GORDON gets up slowly to leave.

SUSAN: Maybe you should have a quick shower first. Just a quick one.

CHRISTINA: Could you imagine? I remember a Van Osch wedding one week, but forget a Frayne wedding the next week. I might as well just ask all the mothers in the county to call in and give me shit.

GORDON grabs the hose on the deck and sprays himself with it.

SUSAN: Gordon, I – and you really should stop all that swearing on the radio, Christina. You know it's not right.

CHRISTINA: But she loves it.

SUSAN: Who loves it?

CHRISTINA: My listeners.

GORDON: Clean.

SUSAN grabs him a new shirt and some shoes.

CHRISTINA: Ten second to air, guys. Are you …?

SUSAN: We're out of here. And do yourself a favour. Page ten.

SUSAN and GORDON exit. CHRISTINA looks at page ten. Her face drops. Light counts down three, two, one.

ACT 1, SCENE 4
STUCK BEHIND A TRACTOR

In the past. CHRISTINA and JASPER are making out.

JASPER: You know what I like a lot?

CHRISTINA: Ruining a moment?

JASPER: No.

CHRISTINA: Because you're pretty good at that.

JASPER: If anybody's good at ruining moments, Chris, that would obviously be you.

CHRISTINA: Oh yeah?

JASPER: Yup, you are.

CHRISTINA: I am not, Jasper, how could you even –

JASPER: But I'm not gonna let you ruin this one. So I'm going to tell you what I like a lot and you're going to listen. Or actually, I can show you. I like sticking my nose right here.

JASPER sticks his nose in CHRISTINA's eye socket.

CHRISTINA: In my eye socket?

JASPER: It fits.

CHRISTINA: Which means?

JASPER: I don't know what it means, but I like it.

CHRISTINA: I like it too.

JASPER: Are you – I mean – how are you feeling?

CHRISTINA: Eh. Jasper.

JASPER: No. Hold on here.

CHRISTINA: I just, I really don't want to –

JASPER: Look, I know this is a weird time for this, but today's been making me think a lot about the moments, you know?

CHRISTINA: Okay.

JASPER: And the time between the moments.

CHRISTINA: Like the space-time continuum?

JASPER: And I'm thinking about you. And Iceland.

CHRISTINA: Iceland? Jasper, what the hell are you doing?

JASPER: Christina Marley.

CHRISTINA: Yes?

JASPER: I don't want to have any moments or any moments between the moments without you. Will you marry me?

CHRISTINA: What?

JASPER: Would you? I want to marry you. I think I always have since you convinced me to play with you in the sand out there when we were six and then you forced me up here with you for dinner and my parents thought I went missing, but then they still drove me out here all the time anyway, every day I wanted them to, and I wanted them to a lot.

CHRISTINA: I can't – Why would you ask me to marry you?

JASPER: We can't?

CHRISTINA: I can't – not today – it's just not right –

JASPER: We can. We should.

CHRISTINA: I can't marry you.

    NADINE enters.

NADINE: Hey guys. I'm here. I'm sorry, I had to make sure the caterer knows where they're going and that they wouldn't serve any cilantro with anything. Can you imagine? Oh! And the flower guy wanted to do all these colourful flowers, so obviously I made him do it all white. It's not usual to add that much colour. It'll look better this way.

CHRISTINA: Great.

JASPER: Sounds good, kiddo.

NADINE: You're not dressed.

CHRISTINA: What?

JASPER: Oh. Yeah.

NADINE: You need to get dressed.

CHRISTINA: We don't need to do anything.

JASPER: We didn't want to get the clothes all dirty, you know?

CHRISTINA: Did you bring out the wine?

NADINE: Yup. Here. I think it's a good choice.

CHRISTINA: I'll be the judge of that.

NADINE: No, no, no. We need to have a quick practice right now, so don't –

CHRISTINA starts drinking the wine.

CHRISTINA: And this will help! With everything.

NADINE: So I was thinking we could play all the, you know, pretty ones.

CHRISTINA: What pretty ones?

NADINE: The pretty songs we have, like "Salt" and "Trees" and –

JASPER: That makes sense. We do have some silly songs that aren't necessarily the best choice for today.

NADINE: Exactly.

CHRISTINA: And I think those are the ones that we should play.

NADINE: But they aren't the usual songs you play, Chris.

CHRISTINA: Well yeah, and? She wasn't usual.

JASPER: No, she wasn't.

CHRISTINA: And she wouldn't want usual songs, trust me.

NADINE: But it's not respectful.

CHRISTINA: Then it's perfect! Look Nadine, I know you want to do something nice, but I think we should do something she would actually like. I think she'll want to get a kick out of it all, don't you?

NADINE: A kick out of it?

CHRISTINA: Uh. Come on. You know what I mean.

JASPER: Chris.

CHRISTINA: What?

NADINE: You can't just say whatever you want all the time.

JASPER: Exactly.

CHRISTINA: It's the right thing to do. What would she want?

NADINE: So you wanna play all the silly ones, like play "On a Highway Stuck behind a Tractor"?

CHRISTINA: That's her absolute favourite.

JASPER: It is her favourite.

NADINE: I know it's her favourite.

JASPER: We could try to make it pretty, Nadine.

CHRISTINA: We have to play it and you know we have to play it. It's for her, not you.

NADINE: How would we make that song even remotely pretty?

JASPER: Uh. Wait. Here. I'll start.
(*singing*) On the highway stuck behind a tractor
I need to get to you on time.
At the chapel wearing your white dress
They warned you I would be unkind.

NADINE and CHRISTINA:
(*singing*) At the Goderich Huron County Museum
A room full of little white dresses
For the tiny Huron County ladies
Getting hitched like they knew they would.

JASPER: (*singing*) On the highway stuck behind a tractor

I need to get to you on time.
Your momma wearing the flowers
Your daddy still holdin' your heart.

NADINE and **CHRISTINA:**
(*singing*) At the Goderich Huron County Museum
A room full of little white dresses
For the tiny Huron County ladies
Getting hitched like they knew they would.

JASPER:
(*singing*) On the highway stuck behind a tractor
I need to get to you on time.
At the chapel wearing your white dress
They warned you I would be unkind,
On the highway suck behind a tractor
I need to get to you on time.
At the chapel wearing ...

NADINE:
(*singing*) My white dress
They warned me you would be unkind.
They warned me you would be unkind.

CHRISTINA goes into a trance. NADINE is crying.

NADINE: Okay. I'm convinced. That was really pretty.

JASPER: Super pretty.

CHRISTINA: I'll be right back.

JASPER: Chris?

CHRISTINA exits to the deck and looks out at the sky, caught somewhere between the past and the present.

JASPER: You okay, Nadine?

NADINE: Do you think we can do the same thing for "Goderich Song"?

JASPER: I don't know, it's a little, it's different –

NADINE: Yeah. Today's hard.

JASPER: It is hard.

> *SUSAN enters in the present, unseen by JASPER and NADINE.*

SUSAN and CHRISTINA: Look at those clouds.

NADINE: Oh whoa. Time. We gotta get out of here. So do we know what we're playing?

JASPER: Well, there's "On a Highway Stuck behind a Tractor."

NADINE: And "Salt" and "Trees." That's enough, right?

JASPER: Yeah. I think so.

NADINE: I think so, too.

JASPER: Okay.

NADINE: So put on your shirt and shoes and we'll get out of here.

JASPER: Yup. Okay.

NADINE: Chris?

CHRISTINA: Yeah.

NADINE: Your clothes, Chris.

CHRISTINA: What about them?

JASPER: Chris, you gotta change.

NADINE: It's time to go.

CHRISTINA: Oh.

NADINE: So, let's go.

CHRISTINA: I, uh – I don't think I will.

NADINE: What?

CHRISTINA: I'm not going.

JASPER: Look, this is going to be hard for everybody here, Chris.

CHRISTINA: I said I'm not going.

NADINE: But the songs, you were right. She would have liked them. We need to play them for her.

CHRISTINA: She's already heard them.

JASPER: Chris.

CHRISTINA: I'm not going.

NADINE: Well, what are you going to do then?

CHRISTINA: Not go. Sit here, I guess.

NADINE: Of course you are.

JASPER: Chris.

NADINE: Somehow this becomes about you.

JASPER: Nadine, it's not an easy day.

NADINE: I know.

CHRISTINA: I'm not going.

NADINE: Well, I'm going. Are you going?

JASPER: I'm going.

NADINE: Looks like it's just you here, on your own then, not going to Mom's funeral.

CHRISTINA: Looks like it.

SUSAN: The clouds.

JASPER: Chris, I think you should –

NADINE: What are you looking at?

SUSAN and CHRISTINA: The clouds.

NADINE: Jasper, we got to get going.

JASPER: Chris, come on.

CHRISTINA: I'm looking at the clouds.

NADINE and JASPER exit.

Lights change. In the present, we hear the sound of rain, which turns into the sound of hail and then turns into the sound of a tornado.

Act 2

ACT 2, SCENE 1
STORM

Present day in the cottage. CHRISTINA is at the radio station. It is the day after the tornado.

CHRISTINA: Hello, *Cottage Radio*.

JOANNE: Chris, I'm so glad I got through. Am I on the air?

CHRISTINA: You are.

JOANNE: This is Joanne Reel from Park Street.

CHRISTINA: Hi, Joanne. Are you – everyone okay?

JOANNE: Well, yes. Mostly.

CHRISTINA: Your house?

JOANNE: Well, it's, uh ...

CHRISTINA: Do you need to publicly report any damage to your property?

JOANNE: Well, there is that, I suppose, but I was hoping –

CHRISTINA: Yeah?

JOANNE: Any chance I can thank some people?

CHRISTINA: You want to thank some people?

JOANNE: It's just, I don't know everyone's names, so I thought maybe over the radio they'd hear it?

CHRISTINA: I, well I guess so –

JOANNE: Well, there are a lot of people to thank, you know, my dad, mom, and my husband, of course. Oh and Earl, my husband's boss. Because we didn't know what was happening when it happened, you know. But when I called Earl, he flew over with Luke in the truck right away. I gotta thank him so much for that!

CHRISTINA: Okay.

JOANNE: And there were these five guys, these guys who were marching around the neighbourhood, you must have seen them, with axes and shovels in their hands, because no cars can get through yet on my street because of the stuff all over the road, and they just came right over and took the tree off the roof. I couldn't believe it. They didn't hardly say anything to me, I was just holding Riley in my arms on the lawn, they just came over and did it.

CHRISTINA: Yeah?

JOANNE: I was sure I would have to hire somebody, you know? But they just did it and didn't even ask for any money or my name or anything. They just went on to the next house with their axes.

CHRISTINA: That's so nice. I'm sure they appreciate you –

JOANNE: I was doing a puzzle with Riley when the power went out.

CHRISTINA: Oh Joanne, I'm not sure it's a great idea to –

JOANNE: I thought it was just a storm, but with the power out and the wind picking up ... I heard a tree hit the yard. Bang! Jesus that was a shock. I went to find my phone to call Luke. Then I heard another tree drop, this time, well my god, right over the living room. I was so scared. Riley in there with the puzzle.

CHRISTINA: I can imagine. But are you sure you want to talk about this over the radio?

MARCUS: I couldn't get the fucking dog to go into the basement.

CHRISTINA: Okay.

MARCUS: And I was so angry at her for whining so much. We trained her for this, you know. Literally drilled her by shaking the table and slamming doors. Even in thunderstorms we trained her, and she did it so well. She was so well behaved. Understood the path to the basement from wherever in the house the drill started, quick fired down the stairs, tucked in next to the washing machine.

CHRISTINA: Did she, Marcus? I mean –

MARCUS: But then the real thing came and she didn't do a damn thing. Stiffened up and howled and whined and forced me to drag her across our carpeted floor, shove her down the stairs, and pack her in next to the washer. The real thing came and she wasn't ready.

CHRISTINA: I'm – I'm sorry.

LAURIE ANNE: Well, my husband Frank's always been a bit, I don't know, I wouldn't say bizarre, but I heard this woman at Zehrs say that once, and I wouldn't say it, but I think other people might see him that way from time to time.

CHRISTINA: Okay.

LAURIE ANNE: He's interested in things the rest of us aren't. It must be from the air force, I don't think – that place doesn't teach you people skills. What I say is, I tell people he can do anything you ask him to around the house, anything, truly.

CHRISTINA: Right, but –

LAURIE ANNE: And he, well he knows a lot about staying tidy, the man still makes our bed every morning, my god, and probably spends more time in the bathroom than I do. He takes pride in everything, including his appearance. But don't expect to know what he's about to say, he's got a lot going on in that head of his and it doesn't always come out in a way that's easy to understand. You know what I mean, Christina?

CHRISTINA: I – Well, I mean I think I do, but –

MARCUS: We're the only family on this side of the block that doesn't live in a heritage home. I opted for a new one, with the grey siding. My mom just about murdered me for not picking a place with antique parts. "Carpets!" I remember her screaming. Creaking old wood floors are the only thing she thought was acceptable, my mom.

CHRISTINA: There are a lot of beautiful old homes in town.

MARCUS: But she shut up when my new roof stayed on and my new foundation stayed strong. She shut up then when neighbour after neighbour picked up their beautiful old yellow bricks off their driveways and saw straight through their houses into the upstairs washrooms or bedrooms or whatever. She shut up then.

CHRISTINA: I see.

LAURIE ANNE: During World War II, Frank was a pilot in the RCAF. He went to PEI once for a course on astral navigation. He'd tell anybody who would let him that he got to take meteorology, celestial navigation, wireless, coding, Morse code, Aldis lamp, calculable navigation, aircraft and ship recognition. I still can't pretend I get what most of that is, really.

CHRISTINA: Laurie Anne –

LAURIE ANNE: But when we went down to the lake for the day because of the family picnic, I was talking to Heather, his sister, and she gives me this look like, oh, he's at it again, Frank's being what some people might call "strange." And I look at Frank and he's just staring up at the sky. Now this is normal for him, I mean the sky's where he feels most comfortable, sometimes I think, so he likes to look up there, so I wasn't all that surprised.

CHRISTINA: Looking at the sky?

LAURIE ANNE: Frank sitting there, staring up at the sky. His sister smiled at me, you know, just because we're friends now, but she smiled at me when Frank said, still staring at the sky, "This is a perfect example of a cold front." Which, well now we know, turns into a tornado, of course.

CHRISTINA: Of course.

TOM: So I was at the harbour, on the freighter, the one loading salt from the mine. I'm, you know, newer to the job so I don't totally know what I'm doing yet. My wife, Sab, Sabrina, makes fun of me because I mostly get paid to watch other people work these days. She calls me a professional eyeball. I am, I guess, for now.

CHRISTINA: Okay.

TOM: The shift started out real good because they were finally giving my hands something to do along with my eyeballs. Nothing major, but more than usual, anyway. It's all super-technical though, more technical than most people realize, maybe. That's what people don't get, and it takes some concentration.

CHRISTINA: Oh yeah.

TOM: We were busy trying to stay on schedule, we just started really getting things going when we heard it, felt it, too. This huge roar came from over the lake. I mean, no bad weather, nothing leading up to it. I wasn't sure what the hell was going on. I thought it was the engine, somehow. It's weird the things your brain tries to get you to believe before the truth. Engines don't make noises like that, you know. And then smack! The wind caught us hard and fuck!

CHRISTINA: Jesus.

TOM: I was inside, but it felt like I was outside. Glass was breaking all fucking around me. The air was full of shit everywhere. Sheet-metal roofing, plywood, insulation, gravel, plus the hail. I couldn't see it all that well, though, 'cause of how dark it got. Everything felt fast, and then the boat caught up with us. We all started to tip forward. Where I was standing began rising slowly out of the water.

CHRISTINA: Oh my god.

TOM: It was like somebody was picking up the ship with a giant hand, lifting this huge hunk of metal like we weighed nothing at all. I swear we stayed like that for a good minute tipping forward until, well, until we weren't.

CHRISTINA: Shit.

TOM: Somehow I was still standing though, all through this, and I looked over at my supervisor. Now, he's a good guy, the kind of guy you wish could be everybody's goddamn dad, but he was leaning over in a weird way. Did he just hit his head? I was super fucking worried, and I knew we had to get out of there, but then wind hit us – Boom! – from the other side this time, more windows breaking into us. Jesus fuck!

CHRISTINA: No.

TOM: I know this sounds impossible, but I swear the next thing felt like the whole goddamn boat was suspended in the fucking air, like that hand grabbed us clean out of the water and was playing with us up there. I thought we might just stay up in the air forever.

CHRISTINA: Oh my god.

TOM: My supervisor grabbed me and pulled me to the ground.
I heard the smash of metal hitting metal five feet from where we
were standing. And then the wind just fucking stopped. I was
so surprised when it was clear the boat was still in the water.
I guess I was so confused while it was all happening, I somehow
hallucinated our ride through the sky. It was my supervisor that
ended up looking at me like I hit my head when I told him.

CHRISTINA: Jesus.

TOM: It took them a while to get us out of there. Sabrina met me
at the emergency room and she looked worried, too, but besides
some cuts and bruises I'm all fine. My supervisor was fine, too.
The emergency nurses said god must have owed us a favour, but
I don't know about that.

JOANNE: Chris?

CHRISTINA: Yeah?

JOANNE: One of those guys with the axes, Chris, he said Riley
was super-lucky to be alive. The tree was right on the roof just
over where she was standing in the living room. It was a huge
maple and would have crushed her if it wasn't stopped by this
lilac bush on its way, holding it up. I almost hit him when the
guy showed it to me. That spring when it was in bloom, every
day Riley told me about how she loved that lilac. How pretty
the purple was, how nice it smelled. And that lilac bush held the
maple balanced there on that roof until those guys appeared out
of nowhere with their axes to take it down.

CHRISTINA: That's – I'm –

JOANNE: It's just that it's in these times we need to thank
people, you know?

CHRISTINA: I, uh –

JOANNE: I just want to know everyone is appreciated for helping.

CHRISTINA: Yeah. Okay.

ACT 2, SCENE 2
SALT

In the past. JASPER, NADINE, and CHRISTINA play "Salt."

NADINE:
    (*singing*) Did you want to tell me why
    You look for me in the sky
    When below the water
    Sits my mother
    And my bitter-tasting lullaby?

    Who didn't tell you
    We've already been through
    The most of this
    The truth of this
    Eyes off the skies?

    Dig holes under the lake
    With metal forks and plates
    In search of me
    Getaway spree.

    Sunk hard like I was salt.
    Sunk hard like I was salt.

ACT 2, SCENE 3

SUSAN

SUSAN is out of space and time, sort of speaking to the audience.

SUSAN: I had a grandmother too, you know. Her name was even Susan, like me. I was upset when their mother didn't name one of them Susan, but I didn't say a word. She wasn't like that, for tradition I mean, and I thought that was good, a positive change in her generation, but I guess I couldn't have known she would stay angry and wild for so long. Christine and Nadine. Pretty names, though. She had taste, their Mom, she had that.

Susan, my grandmother, was tall, tall like a bean. On stilts, we all thought, but god, she was mean. She'd tell you you were ugly if she thought it, and she thought it often enough. She had the decency to say it in Latin, though, which she spoke quite well, us being Catholic. I heard that a few times. It kept you pretty, though, thinking you were ugly all the time.

God, Susan must have found it fun saying what she thought in a language hardly anybody could understand. Meaner and meaner she got there in that home. Their mom thought it was hilarious and would bring anybody in there who could understand it. Her school friends, mostly, but then, well, she went too far, like usual, and brought in Father Pluta. Now that priest almost had a heart attack when Susan started in on him in Latin. My crazy daughter was laughing so hard. She always laughed at the most uncomfortable things. Poor Father Pluta hadn't heard such colourful phrasing in Latin before, I can't imagine. Grandma was creative. ·

I think I would say something now to my daughter if I could do it again. I would if I knew then how she wouldn't grow out of it. It's not that it's my name, but that's it's her name, Susan, maybe if one of them had it then I could help see into their future a little bit.

Act 3

ACT 3, SCENE 1
COCOA PUFFS

The present. 3 a.m. at the cottage. CHRISTINA is asleep on the couch. Headlights are seen through the window. A car door opens and shuts. NADINE enters with a bag and a guitar. She sees CHRISTINA asleep on the couch. NADINE puts her things down and has a quick look around. CHRISTINA wakes up and sees NADINE. CHRISTINA gets off the bed and hides. NADINE turns around to see CHRISTINA is gone. She looks concerned. CHRISTINA comes up behind NADINE and scares her. NADINE screams and CHRISTINA tackles her to the ground, covering her mouth and laughing. They speak in loud whispers.

NADINE: You monster!

CHRISTINA: Hi, Nadine.

NADINE: Chris, why can't you just say hello like a normal person? Just a regular old hello. And give me a hug, maybe?

CHRIS: That wasn't a good enough hug for ya?

NADINE: No, I –

CHRISTINA: Well, here we go!

> *CHRISTINA tackles NADINE into another hug and the two laugh.*

NADINE: Get off me, you wild woman!

CHRISTINA: I think you liked it.

NADINE: Well, you're wrong. Who else is here right now?

CHRISTINA: Grandma's in the other room.

NADINE: Shit. We should be quiet.

CHRISTINA: I wasn't sure I'd recognize you after the city messed with you, but look at you.

NADINE: What?

CHRISTINA: You're exactly the same.

NADINE: Am I?

CHRISTINA: Except ... Oh my god.

NADINE: What?

CHRISTINA: Your neck.

NADINE: My neck?

CHRISTINA: Your neck ... is fat.

NADINE: My neck is fat?

CHRISTINA: Jesus, this is good.

NADINE: How is it possibly good that my neck got fat?

CHRISTINA: Hey. Somebody like you needs to get fat somewhere every once in a while.

NADINE: I don't think they do.

CHRISTINA: It's good for you.

NADINE: Oh yeah?

CHRISTINA: Neck fat, Nadine, it's good on you.

NADINE: Well, you look –

CHRISTINA: What?

NADINE: Good!

CHRISTINA: Okay, I know I'm fat, too. I'm just glad I'm not the only one.

NADINE: No, I was going to say the opposite, actually –

CHRISTINA: But I'm fat more around here, though, in the typical getting-old-kinda-place for fat. I hate pants now. Where's the French boy?

NADINE: Tomorrow. He couldn't get off work right away, he'll be down tomorrow.

CHRISTINA: So we all get to meet him tomorrow?

NADINE: Yup, tomorrow. Are you guys okay?

CHRISTINA: Ah, here we go.

NADINE: Is everybody okay?

CHRISTINA: Nadine.

NADINE: I honestly, like, really truly came as quickly as I could.

CHRISTINA: Nadine.

NADINE: What do we need to do? How can I help?

CHRISTINA: We're fine.

NADINE: But our house! Grandma told me on the phone. Well, there must be so much cleaning to do and the trees must be everywhere.

CHRISTINA: It was just a little wind.

NADINE: A little wind?

CHRISTINA: What?

NADINE: Chris, a tor-na-do!

CHRISTINA: Jesus.

NADINE: A tornado hit our town.

CHRISTINA: You're so dramatic.

NADINE: It is dramatic. I can't even believe it. It's so
wild. A tornado!

CHRISTINA: It was just a storm.

NADINE: How's Dad taking it?

CHRISTINA: He's ...

NADINE: What?

CHRISTINA: Look, you really didn't have to come if you're just
going to make a big deal out of everything.

NADINE: I heard the whole downtown is ripped up. The old
courthouse destroyed.

CHRISTINA: The courthouse is fine, just some broken glass.

NADINE: There must be so much to do. People in town must need
food, is somebody making them food? I made up some chili
before I left. It's in the car.

CHRISTINA: That's nice, but somebody's taking care of that.

NADINE: And I have some garbage bags and there's cleaning
supplies in the car, too.

CHRISTINA: Nadine.

NADINE: Yeah?

CHRISTINA: It's 3 a.m.

NADINE: Yeah, but –

CHRISTINA: What are you going to do now, lift trees in the dark?

NADINE: I – I don't know.

CHRISTINA: It's been a long while since you've been here.

NADINE: It hasn't been that long.

CHRISTINA: Long enough for you to develop neck fat, anyway.

NADINE: Watch yourself. Okay. So tell me about it then. Were you in town when the tornado came through?

CHRISTINA: I, well – I –

NADINE: Yeah?

CHRISTINA: You jerk!

NADINE: What?

CHRISTINA: That's my fucking sweatshirt, you little shit.

NADINE: What? No it's not.

CHRISTINA: I don't see you for a million years and then you show up wearing my goddamn sweatshirt.

NADINE: Are you sure this is yours?

CHRISTINA: You got some balls. What does it say there on your right boob?

NADINE: "Goderich Tsunami."

CHRISTINA: You little brat. That is my senior-volleyball sweatshirt.

NADINE: I guess I've just had it so long.

CHRISTINA: What a little thief.

NADINE: Would you like it back?

CHRISTINA: I'll fucking pull it right off you if you're not careful. I'll always be older than you, Nadine.

NADINE: It's good to see you, too.

CHRISTINA: Okay.

NADINE: It's good to be home.

CHRISTINA: Am I right in assuming you still eat Cocoa Puffs in the morning?

NADINE: Usually after I've slept a bit but –

CHRISTINA: But?

NADINE: Yes. Occasionally.

CHRISTINA: And am I also right in assuming you continue to ruin Cocoa Puffs with healthy bananas?

NADINE: I absolutely do.

CHRISTINA: Then you might be happy with what's in the kitchen right now.

NADINE: No way!

CHRISTINA: So go grab us some bowls, but make sure mine does not have healthy bananas.

NADINE: It's really good to see you. I thought it might be – but I'm so happy to see you, really.

CHRISTINA: Shut up, you idiot, and get some goddamn cereal, Jesus, don't be so fucking embarrassing.

NADINE exits towards the kitchen. Headlights in the driveway.

CHRISTINA: Hey. Nadine. Nadine! Are we expecting someone else? What time is it? Nadine!

A car door can be heard. CHRISTINA recognizes JASPER coming to the door.

CHRISTINA: Oh. Shit. You gotta be kidding me.

CHRISTINA panics and then goes to exit out to the beach, but can't. CHRISTINA groans loudly.

NADINE enters with the cereal bowls.

NADINE: Oh hey! I forgot to tell you Jasper called and asked if he could stay. I guess this is turning into a little Cottage Radio reunion!

CHRISTINA: Fuuuuck.

NADINE: Chris? Are you –

CHRISTINA: He called you?

NADINE: Yeah.

CHRISTINA: Jasper called you and asked you to stay here?

NADINE: Well, yeah.

CHRISTINA: And you said yes?

NADINE: I just thought you would be okay with it. It's been a while and it's Jasper ...

CHRISTINA: Do I look okay with it?

NADINE: No. You don't.

The door opens and JASPER enters.

JASPER: Nadine!

NADINE: Jasper!

JASPER: You look so happy to see me.

NADINE: I am!

JASPER: Are you, now?

NADINE: I am so happy to see you!

JASPER: Oh, kiddo. I told you this would – where is she?

NADINE points to CHRISTINA.

JASPER: Hi, Chris.

CHRISTINA: Hey there.

JASPER: Okay. It's okay. I'll find somewhere else to stay.

NADINE: I'm sorry I didn't think –

JASPER: No. No. No. It's all good. I'll be fine. Really. There are lots of hotels near here.

NADINE: A hotel? No! That's crazy.

JASPER: It's fine.

CHRISTINA: Why can't you stay at your mom's?

NADINE: You don't know?

JASPER: I thought you would –

NADINE: That's why he's here, wild woman. The place was totalled. Am I right?

JASPER: It's not great. Mom and Dad are over in Wingham with Aunt Jessie.

CHRISTINA: Oh.

JASPER: Well, and I'm here to help you guys out, too. Your parent's place. You guys know I'm always here to help out the beautiful Marley girls.

NADINE: Chris.

CHRISTINA: That's nice.

NADINE: Chris.

CHRISTINA: Yeah, okay, whatever. You can stay. Just don't touch my radio equipment.

NADINE: He won't. Will you?

JASPER: Uh – no.

NADINE: There you go.

CHRISTINA: It's expensive.

JASPER: I can see that. Did you have to pay for it yourself?

CHRISTINA: No. The station pays for it.

JASPER: That's nice of them.

NADINE: Look, Jasper, why don't you take the couch. Chris and I'll take the spare bedroom. Okay, Chris?

CHRISTINA: I don't like sleeping in the spare bedroom.

NADINE: But you will for one night, won't ya?

CHRISTINA: Don't you want your Cocoa Puffs?

NADINE: What? Oh, I, uh – I don't know. Do you want your Cocoa Puffs, Chris?

CHRISTINA: I asked you first.

NADINE: I, well, I –

JASPER: Still eat them with bananas?

NADINE laughs.

NADINE: You know me!

CHRISTINA: You know, I don't think I am hungry for Cocoa Puffs.

NADINE: Okay.

JASPER: Chris, I ...

CHRISTINA: What?

NADINE: Okay. Well, I wanted to have an early start so I could get into town and help in the morning and it's already almost morning so –

CHRISTINA: It's sleeping time.

> *CHRISTINA exits into the bedroom with her bowl of Cocoa Puffs.*

NADINE: Goodnight, Jasper.

JASPER: Night.

> *NADINE exits into the bedroom, and JASPER lies down on the couch. JASPER sighs. GORDON enters from the beach carrying a paddle. He is wet.*

GORDON: This is my paddle.

JASPER: I see that. Went for a late-night cruise on the lake, did ya, Gordie?

GORDON: The photos in the album. Did they get in the water?

JASPER: I don't know.

> *GORDON lies down holding his paddle.*

JASPER: Gordie, would you – do you need a blanket or something?

GORDON: My paddle and paddle and paddle and paddle.

JASPER: Okay. All right.

> *JASPER puts a blanket over GORDON and tries to go to sleep on the couch.*

JASPER: Jesus.

ACT 3, SCENE 2
MEMORIAL

*Spotlight on JANE. As she speaks, the cottage fades in
around her. It is around 1 p.m. CHRISTINA is on the radio.
GORDON periodically enters carrying wood up from the
beach and places it on the deck.*

JANE: A lot of people go golfing, but I like to walk the old-
fashioned way, for no reason at all. Just to listen to the birds
and look at the trees, let my dog sniff some grass. Most days I
walk past the golf course, though, because some of my family
runs the place, and I usually stop to say hi to whoever is around.
That day, I really should have planned to golf with the rest of
them, probably. There was the Golf Scramble and Dinner going
on. They do it every year, but it was special that day. I'll admit,
a ninety-year anniversary is an achievement. I mean, that
doesn't happen every day. Ninety whole years.

CHRISTINA: That's a lot o' years.

JANE: The morning was wet, but I guess they decided to go out
anyway because by the time I walked down around three thirty,
the course was full. My cousin's foursome was there, and we
chatted a minute while they got ready to set out. It's funny,
because Darlene actually kind of hates golf, too. You know how
it is, she runs the club, so she should be good at it, and she is
and all, but she can't be too good, because then the members
complain they can't win, and it's a real head game sometimes,
and then there's the times where she's not good at all and then
they really get angry, saying she's not even trying, which ticks
her off, especially when she is tryin'. And she can't not go out at
all like me, obviously. Then they'd really have something to say.
But by the time I got there, I think she thought she might be
saved because of the dark clouds.

CHRISTINA: But let me guess, she wasn't?

NADINE enters from the bedroom in her pyjamas and stands listening to the story.

JANE: I joked with her, "You arranged this, didn't you? Got those clouds here because you didn't feel like going out today?" She laughed but clearly wanted my bad attitude out of there. She reminded me how some people really care about the anniversary. Ninety years. She said I should really be out there with the rest of them. But no way. Not me.

CHRISTINA: Uh-huh.

JANE: And especially not under those clouds. I headed back, taking my pup home. Then, so I could get home faster, I walked straight up the hill from there. It was really raining by then, dark, windy. At the top of the hill, I looked down and just barely made out Darlene's pink shirt darting through the course to get inside. I thought about hiding under a tree.

CHRISTINA: Under a tree? Look, Jane –

JANE: I know, exactly like you shouldn't, so instead I picked up my dog and started to run the rest of the way home.

CHRISTINA: I see, so –

JANE: And Darlene or someone must have gotten inside, because I heard the horn you're supposed to toot to get everybody off the course.

CHRISTINA: Because there was a tornado.

JANE: Well. Uh. Yeah.

CHRISTINA: Okay. And you made it.

JANE: I did.

CHRISTINA: Super. So then tell me, Jane, what do you want to hear?

JANE: Excuse me?

CHRISTINA: What song?

JANE: Song?

CHRISTINA: The radio. This magical broadcast we're waving out on right now all the way out to the Huron County border. What is the song you would like to request to transmit to all those faithful ears listening in right now?

JANE: I didn't really – do I have to make a request, Christina?

CHRISTINA: Not sure? Well, what do you say to a little Sarah Harmer?

JANE: Can't say I've ever heard of her.

CHRISTINA: Oh Janey Jane, you are in for a treat.

JANE: But my story. I'm not done. I thought you were listening to the tornado stories, Chris.

CHRISTINA: Listening. Yeah. I have been listening a lot, haven't I?

JANE: Well. Okay. So then I went inside and –

CHRISTINA: But I'm sorry, Jane.

JANE: Sorry for what? Look, I think it's wonderful that you're letting people call in.

CHRISTINA: Do you?

JANE: It's a great thing to let us do.

CHRISTINA: "Let." I think that's a key word in there, Jane.

JANE: What do you mean?

CHRISTINA: So then guess what?

JANE: What?

CHRISTINA: As appointed radio hostess, I am making the executive decision not to "let" anymore. That this show, well it just needs a little more music and a little less story.

JANE: But you can't just –

CHRISTINA: Were you appointed host of this program, Jane?

JANE: Well no, but –

CHRISTINA: So I can just. And I think I will just, Janey Jane. For the good of us all. Moving on and all that. No tornado can get us down! And I'm afraid that next story that calls in, I just might find that the program isn't in the mood then, either. It's time for music.

JANE: You wouldn't –

CHRISTINA: So here we go, folks! As promised, Ms. Sarah Harmer, "Coffee Stain."

> CHRISTINA pushes a button to turn on the song.
> JANE's spot fades.

NADINE: Well, good morning.

CHRISTINA: Looks like afternoon to me.

NADINE: What? Oh crap. I – did I really sleep that long?

CHRISTINA: Like you haven't slept in years. I actually tried waking you. Your eyes tried to open, but, like, couldn't. It was weird.

GORDON enters with another piece of wood.

NADINE: Oh my god! Hey Dad!

GORDON stares up at NADINE and then goes back to work.

NADINE: What is he ...

CHRISTINA: Building?

NADINE: Yeah.

CHRISTINA: A coffin, probably.

NADINE: What?

CHRISTINA laughs.

NADINE: Okay. Okay. What is he really making?

CHRISTINA: No idea, he came in last night after we went to bed. He was missing for, like, over twenty-four hours, you know.

NADINE: He was? Why didn't anybody tell me?

CHRISTINA: He was at the house and then the tornado and then he wasn't at the house. There, you're told. And now here he is.

NADINE: Oh.

CHRISTINA: As soon as he woke up, this started happening.

NADINE: He looks –

CHRISTINA: Old?

NADINE: No. He –

GORDON: Nadine!

NADINE: Yeah?

GORDON: Grab me a beer.

NADINE: Oh. Uh –

CHRISTINA grabs three beers and NADINE looks confused.

CHRISTINA: Two for him. One for you.

NADINE: No, I –

CHRISTINA: Just take them. Here.

NADINE takes two beers from the three.

NADINE: Just two for him. Thanks.

CHRISTINA: Okay.

NADINE goes outside to GORDON and offers him a beer. CHRISTINA starts drinking inside.

NADINE: Is this okay?

GORDON: Thanks.

NADINE: What are you, uh – can I help?

GORDON: Uh. Yeah.

NADINE: Yeah?

GORDON: See this piece of twine? Circles. Like this.

GORDON shows NADINE how to wrap twine between two pieces of wood.

NADINE: Like this?

GORDON: You got it.

NADINE: I didn't know you were so crafty, Dad.

GORDON: Okay. I'm off for more.

NADINE: Wait! Uh –

GORDON: What?

NADINE: Nothing.

GORDON: Can you handle that?

NADINE: Yeah, I mean – I think so.

GORDON: Good.

GORDON exits to the beach. NADINE attempts to wrap twine around the wood. The song ends.

CHRISTINA: Now wasn't that refreshing, Goderich? Oh no, no. I see your little blinking story lights flashing, but I mean it, folks. No more stories. Moving on! Next song, here we go!

CHRISTINA plays another song. SUSAN enters carrying a box.

SUSAN: Coming through!

CHRISTINA: Jesus, watch it!

SUSAN: Watch yourself, Christina.

NADINE: Grandma!

SUSAN: Oh hello, pretty girl.

NADINE: It's so great to see you! Do you? Can I?

SUSAN: Do I look like I need help carrying this box?

NADINE: No.

CHRISTINA: Good answer.

SUSAN: Did you just get up? You're still in your pyjamas.

NADINE: I guess I slept in. I meant to get up so much earlier.

SUSAN: And what's that? A craft on the deck there?

NADINE: Oh no, that's, well I think it's –

SUSAN: There was a tornado, you know, Nadine. Wouldn't hurt you to help out like the rest of us. Or is this your vacation?

NADINE: I did come to help, actually I'm already helping Dad, with this.

> NADINE shows SUSAN what she was working on. JASPER enters holding a big box.

JASPER: Where do you want this one, Sue?

SUSAN: Jesus, Christina, help him with that.

JASPER: Oh, I'm fine.

CHRISTINA: He says he's fine.

SUSAN: Well, he doesn't look fine.

JASPER: Sue, I said I'm fine. Check this out. (*bench-pressing the box*) One, two, three!

NADINE: Oh. Uh, wow.

CHRISTINA: My hero.

JASPER: Anything to impress a beautiful Marley girl.

SUSAN: Very nice, Jasper. You can put that one over there.

NADINE: All this from the house? Is there more in the car?

JASPER: Loads.

NADINE: I can go grab it.

SUSAN: That would be good.

NADINE: Great.

CHRISTINA: But you were right in the middle of your craft for Dad.

NADINE: Oh, I'm sure –

CHRISTINA: Hey, Grandma, Nadine can finish her craft first before helping, can't she?

NADINE: Chris, I really don't need –

SUSAN: Oh yeah, go back to that if you like, Nadine. Who am I to stop you? With the tornado and all.

NADINE: Oh no. It wasn't. It's Chris. She was –

SUSAN: It doesn't make any difference, Nadine. Jasper and I can empty out the rest of the car. Can't we, Jasper?

JASPER: Sure thing, Sue.

NADINE: But Grandma –

SUSAN: It's okay. That looks important. Back out I go!

NADINE: No, Grandma, you should let me do that.

SUSAN: It's really okay, I mean I don't –

NADINE: I need to grab some other things out of my car, so let me … gimme a minute.

SUSAN: I don't –

NADINE: It'll just take me a minute.

NADINE exits.

JASPER: Chris?

CHRISTINA: Yeah.

JASPER: I see you're still causing shit for your sister.

CHRISTINA: Who, me?

JASPER: Bet you think you're pretty funny.

CHRISTINA: You don't think so?

JASPER: Maybe a little.

SUSAN: Well, she's eager.

CHRISTINA: As opposed to?

SUSAN: You better be nice to her.

CHRISTINA: Why?

SUSAN: I mean it.

CHRISTINA: Come on.

SUSAN: She's a good girl coming home to help, even if she's turned nocturnal now.

CHRISTINA: And I'm not a good girl, Grandma?

SUSAN: Do you really want me to answer that?

JASPER: I do.

CHRISTINA: Well, Nadine showed up wearing a stolen sweatshirt.

SUSAN: What?

JASPER: What sweatshirt?

CHRISTINA: My Goderich Tsunami one. That's from my senior high school volleyball final tournament.

SUSAN: Oh wow. What are you worked up about, Jesus, Christina? Nobody cares about your volleyball tournaments from over a decade ago.

CHRISTINA: I do.

SUSAN: Well, you might try living in the present like the rest of us.

CHRISTINA: Thanks.

SUSAN: Like Jasper here. He doesn't live in the past. He's looking to the future, right Jasper?

JASPER: I guess so.

SUSAN: Well, you are. Anybody who's engaged is looking forward, that's how it goes.

JASPER: Oh.

SUSAN: Well, am I right?

JASPER: You, Sue, are very rarely wrong.

SUSAN: So, the girl, I hear she's foreign.

CHRISTINA: "Foreign." Jesus, Grandma, nobody says "foreign" anymore.

SUSAN: Well, what am I supposed to say?

JASPER: She's from Iceland. Her name is Assa.

SUSAN: So "Icelandic," then. Is that better?

CHRISTINA: Iceland? So you made it out there, then?

JASPER: Six months. Best spot on the trip.

SUSAN: Well, I guess so, coming back with a young bride.

> *NADINE enters carrying a cooler and takes out two pots of chili. CHRISTINA switches the song on the radio.*

SUSAN: And the wedding? Do you have a date?

JASPER: It's in two weeks.

SUSAN: Well that's ...

NADINE: Romantic.

JASPER: Why wait?

SUSAN: Is she ... well, she isn't ... (*indicating pregnant*)

JASPER: Nope. It's just time. I don't want to lose any of it.

SUSAN: Looking to the future. You could learn from
that, Christina.

CHRISTINA: I love learning.

SUSAN: Well congratulations, Jasper. I hope to meet the
lucky girl in person someday. Nadine, what do you have in
those pots there?

NADINE: I made up some chili, Grandma, for everyone.
Brought it here.

SUSAN: That's nice, good girl.

NADINE: I hope I brought enough. I can heat some up now
if anyone is –

SUSAN: I'm starving.

JASPER: Maybe I should get going, you guys could use some
Marley lady time, I'm sure.

SUSAN: No, no. You carry boxes. We feed and house you. That's
the deal. We might as well feed him before he runs away
to Iceland for good, right girls?

NADINE: Okay, great! Give me a few minutes while I heat up your
pot, Grandma. I'll do that one first.

SUSAN: My pot? Why do I get a whole pot to myself?

NADINE: Well, I put together a meat pot and a vegetarian pot.

SUSAN: And which pot is mine?

NADINE: Well, uh –

SUSAN: Which pot is mine?

CHRISTINA: Did you bring vegetarian chili just for Grandma, Nadine?

JASPER: Chris –

NADINE: Well, if anybody else wants some I'm happy to heat some up for everybody. There should be enough, maybe. It's for everyone, really.

SUSAN: Who said I can't eat meat?

NADINE: Nobody. Nobody said that.

CHRISTINA: I would certainly not say that and expect to keep my life.

JASPER: I'm sure she's just being thoughtful, Sue.

SUSAN: How is that thoughtful?

JASPER: Well, nobody should eat too much red meat, right Nadine?

SUSAN: Is that right, Nadine?

CHRISTINA: Why can't Grandma eat red meat, Nadine?

NADINE: I, well, I –

SUSAN: Go ahead.

NADINE: Well, um, it has been tested that women of a certain age need a little extra help cleaning out that area.

CHRISTINA: Fucking hell, Nadine. "That area?"

SUSAN: You know what else women my age need?

NADINE: Grandma, I didn't mean –

SUSAN: Naps. Don't you think? Just put me to bed, but help me, because I probably can't make it there myself, I'm too old.

NADINE: I didn't say –

SUSAN: Just try to wake me up when I'm dead. Shouldn't be too far away. Just set the alarm.

NADINE: No! I didn't mean –

SUSAN: And you all might as well know that "that area" is working just fine, thank you.

NADINE: Grandma!

CHRISTINA and JASPER laugh.

CHRISTINA: Excellent.

JASPER: You just had to provoke this.

CHRISTINA: I think she might be responsible for this one on her own.

SUSAN: My poo, my excrement, is coming out of me and going into the toilet bowl just fine.

CHRISTINA: Oh my god.

JASPER: Atta girl, Sue.

NADINE: Please, Grandma, I –

SUSAN: I am not constipated. I do not need extra-special foods. I eat what I like to eat and send it packing when I'm done with it. Got it?

NADINE: Got it.

JASPER: Oh, we got it.

CHRISTINA: I'm so happy right now.

SUSAN: You eat what you want, don't you? You're the ones that are young and can still change things, what should I try to change for? You're young. You change! I'm heading back to town where I'm needed. Jasper, let's go into town. There was a tornado, if you haven't forgotten. No, no. Just sit around and play make-believe on the radio or crafts in the corner instead of doing something productive, helpful. Just enjoy that delicious meat chili on your own there, kids. I wouldn't want to burden you with my old-lady ways. It's no use. I'm no use to either of you.

JASPER and SUSAN exit. The song is ending.

CHRISTINA: Nadine.

NADINE: What?

CHRISTINA: (*on air*) Say hi to the folks of Huron County, Sis.

NADINE shakes her head.

CHRISTINA: Come on, Goderich, you want to hear from her, don't ya? Let's give her a little encouragement. Nadine, Nadine, Nadine.

NADINE: (*on air*) Um. Hello, *Cottage Radio*, Nadine speaking.

CHRISTINA: We should put you on our answering machine.

NADINE: Oh. Uh. Sorry. I just –

CHRISTINA: You wanna try again?

NADINE: What? Saying hello?

CHRISTINA: Go ahead, the people won't mind, will you, Goderich?

NADINE: Hey, Goderich, how's it hanging?

CHRISTINA: Better.

NADINE: Really?

CHRISTINA: We'll take it, won't we, Goderich?

NADINE: Is that a caller?

CHRISTINA: What? Oh no.

NADINE: It's not? I thought –

CHRISTINA: Well, it is a caller, Nadine, but we already got one guest on the program, my baby sister. Can't the Marley sisters have a conversation without the rest of you interrupting us, Goderich?

NADINE: Maybe they want to talk about the tornado.

CHRISTINA: Eh –

NADINE: I think we should.

CHRISTINA: Okay, so fine. You might as well answer the question swirling around the county then, Sis.

NADINE: Me?

CHRISTINA: Where were you when the tornado came through?

NADINE: Well, not here.

CHRISTINA: No. I don't remember you in the cottage.

NADINE: Or the county.

CHRISTINA: But in the province.

NADINE: In Toronto. Where I live now.

CHRISTINA: So I'm sure our listeners are imagining you just hanging out at the CN Tower, or in the SkyDome or a streetcar or something. But that's not where you were?

NADINE: I was at my place and I was –

CHRISTINA: Your place? As in your apartment?

NADINE: Yes. With François.

CHRISTINA: The French boy.

NADINE: That's the one.

CHRISTINA: Is he still planning on –

NADINE: Tomorrow. You'll meet him tomorrow.

CHRISTINA: Do the listeners a favour and describe your apartment. For our listeners.

NADINE: My apartment. Well. It's small, not Toronto-small, but Goderich-small, as in if anyone from around here were living in it, you'd think there was something wrong with them, but in Toronto, it's normal to live in something so small. White walls and white-tile floor.

CHRISTINA: It's part of a house?

NADINE: The basement, there's a family upstairs. So when
   the tornado –

CHRISTINA: How many bedrooms?

NADINE: One.

CHRISTINA: Is the kitchen and the living room all one space
   or are they –

NADINE: I'm not sure why Goderich is so curious, exactly, but yes.
   We're lucky to have a separate bedroom, most people I know
   live in a square of space and that's it, you eat there, you live
   there, you sleep there.

CHRISTINA: You've met a lot of people.

NADINE: Cities have lots of them.

CHRISTINA: So how did the tornado even get on your radar over
   here in insignificant land?

NADINE: It was on the news there, it's a big deal
   everywhere, I mean –

CHRISTINA: So that's how you hear about it? The news?

NADINE: Not the traditional news, I guess.

CHRISTINA: What do you mean?

NADINE: My news feed. On Facebook. This girl I went to high
   school with, she posted about it. Honestly, I haven't talked to
   her in years, but I've been, um, reading what she's been up to
   a lot lately.

CHRISTINA: So you've been stalking this girl?

NADINE: Sort of! I've been following her because she just had a baby and I see her baby on Facebook all the time now. I like seeing the families that form around here, so I've been spying on her and her baby and her husband and her dog a lot lately. It's reassuring to know she has a baby and is living her life somehow.

CHRISTINA: And she posted about the tornado?

NADINE: It was in the form of a note to god thanking him for making sure her family got through the storm safely. She posted a picture of the courthouse mess to go along with it.

CHRISTINA: Wow.

NADINE: It made me feel really alone. And guilty, for not being here.

CHRISTINA: But you're here now, and you brought chili.

NADINE: Chris!

CHRISTINA: She brought chili, folks, all the way from the CN Tower.

NADINE: It's just chili. I was trying to be thoughtful.

CHRISTINA: It is thoughtful.

NADINE: I brought a guitar, too.

CHRISTINA: I hadn't noticed.

NADINE: Can I make a request?

CHRISTINA: A song request?

NADINE: If you're feeling up for it, we could –

CHRISTINA: Wow, I didn't know we were going to torture Goderich today. We haven't played together in a while, sis, and you want to broadcast it on the radio.

NADINE: I think we can handle it.

CHRISTINA: There must be a recording of a song that would satisfy our listeners.

NADINE: But it's my request you're granting, not theirs.

CHRISTINA: Which song are you feeling?

NADINE: Wanna go swimming?

CHRISTINA: Oh, Jesus. I thought you were going to pick a good song.

NADINE: That *is* a good song!

CHRISTINA: So Nadine and I used to sing this very silly song at the beach all the time when we were little kids.

NADINE: Our first original song.

CHRISTINA: Jesus!

NADINE: It was good enough for us then.

CHRISTINA: You sure you want to do this?

NADINE: Chris, count me in.

CHRISTINA and NADINE sing the song "Sand."

CHRISTINA and NADINE:
    (*singing*) Water handstands
    Tidal splish-splashes
    Dolphin dives

And king of the air mattress
Shark tag
Stiff-board float
Shoulder dives
And playing motorboat, motorboat
That first spring swim

Is really all about
Finding the sandbar at the beach!

Swimming little cousins
Out to the spot
Grab them by the waist
And throw, slingshot
That first spring swim

Is really all about
Finding the sandbar at the beach!

Oh no, here he comes
Dad with his beer
The sandbar ain't big enough
When he's here
Playing one-handed volleyball
Lake sure to get drunk
Drops a-flying all around
He's almost sunk
Towel hot on the sand
Sun beams from up high
His drink shadows
A beer tanned to his side
That first spring swim

Is really all about
Finding the sandbar at the beach!

CHRISTINA: For putting up with that song, Goderich ...

NADINE: It's a good song.

CHRISTINA: ... you now get to listen to a real old-fashioned recorded song.

NADINE: You're really not going to take one of these callers?

CHRISTINA: And go!

> CHRISTINA *pushes a button.*

NADINE: Do you think Grandma will ever forgive me?

CHRISTINA: That woman is not really mad at you.

NADINE: She seems mad.

CHRISTINA: It's been a while since you were here.

NADINE: I don't think I can go back to Toronto with her like this.

CHRISTINA: Back to Toronto.

NADINE: Yeah.

CHRISTINA: That's happening soon?

NADINE: Well, yeah. No. I don't know. It is where I live.

> CHRISTINA *gets a beer.*

CHRISTINA: You know, she's more than just our grandma.

NADINE: What do you mean?

CHRISTINA: Susan Marley.

NADINE: Okay.

CHRISTINA: Beer?

NADINE: No, I'm okay. This cottage is really wonderful. You know, I think you might have it right hanging out here all day.

CHRISTINA: Do I?

NADINE: Look how beautiful this is.

CHRISTINA: Yeah. You sure you don't want a beer?

NADINE: No, thank you. You like living here, don't you, Chris?

CHRISTINA: Like you said, it's beautiful.

NADINE: Well, you don't have to live here.

CHRISTINA: I don't?

NADINE: Of course you don't. There's a lot out there.

CHRISTINA: A lot of what?

NADINE: People. Places.

CHRISTINA: A lot of people and places.

NADINE: Yeah. I don't know.

CHRISTINA: We saw a lot of people and places when we were touring. That's enough for me.

NADINE: How often do you visit Mom's plot?

CHRISTINA: I – I don't know.

NADINE: I haven't been since I left. How screwed up is that?

CHRISTINA: So screwed up.

NADINE: Okay.

CHRISTINA: Well, you asked.

NADINE: I did ask.

CHRISTINA: Uh. Another fucking caller.

NADINE: Yeah.

CHRISTINA: Hang up, will you?

NADINE: Shouldn't we see what they want?

CHRISTINA: We don't have to.

NADINE: I know. It's your show.

CHRISTINA: Ehhh.

NADINE: What.

CHRISTINA: Just ... take the call if you want.

NADINE: Hello, *Cottage Radio*.

LEO: Am I on the air?

NADINE: No, there's a song on right now. Is there a story you want to share?

LEO: Not exactly. More like a notice.

CHRISTINA: Thank god.

NADINE: What kind of notice?

LEO: For the memorial.

CHRISTINA: Oh.

LEO: It's happening this weekend, so I want to get the word out if I can?

NADINE: I didn't know anybody died.

CHRISTINA: At the salt mine. Leo, is that you?

LEO: It is.

CHRISTINA: Email over the notice and Nadine will read it on the air.

LEO: Okay.

NADINE: Me? Why would you want me to read the notice?

LEO: It's sent over. Thanks, Chris.

CHRISTINA: See ya, Leo.

NADINE: I really don't think that I'm the right person to read this.

CHRISTINA: You wanted to take the call, didn't you? You have three seconds to air. Here's Leo's email.

NADINE: Welcome back to the *Cottage Radio* program. I have a notice that I'd like to read for you all, so please listen in:

A memorial service will be held for Normand J. Laberge of RR number seven, Lucknow, on Friday, August 26, 2011. Mr. Laberge passed away suddenly as a result of an accident in Goderich on August 21, 2011, at the age of sixty-one. Beloved husband of Brenda Turcotte-Laberge. Father of Mary-Louise Laberge and Jocelyn (*Michael*) Cockburn. Grandfather of Franklin Cockburn. Survived by stepsons Shaun and Arden Laird and their children Megan, Morgan, Macheala, Brianna, Aaron, and Dylan. Also greatly missed by mother Ruth Laberge (*Morrow*), brother Richard Laberge, sister Johane Laberge, and father-in-law David Turcotte and family. Predeceased by father Maurice Laberge.

CHRISTINA offers NADINE another beer, and NADINE accepts this time.

ACT 3, SCENE 3
ROT

The present. 8 p.m. at the cottage. CHRISTINA and NADINE have been drinking most of the afternoon. NADINE is pretty drunk. JASPER has been working most of the day and is tired but settling into his old life with the Marleys. SUSAN feels as though she put in a good day in town and wants to try to help resolve things for her family. GORDON is finished his raft.

CHRISTINA: Okay. Time for the real cottage experience. Here we go. Ready? One. Two. Three!

CHRISTINA, NADINE, and JASPER punch their beer cans with scissors and shotgun their beers at the same time.

CHRISTINA: And chase with a shot of tequila!

NADINE: Oh my god.

JASPER: Whoop!

CHRISTINA: You up for it, old man?

JASPER: Gordie, you don't have to –

CHRISTINA: Yes, he does. It's family tradition, and I think he's family.

NADINE: I don't see Grandma being this stupid.

SUSAN: Well, I wouldn't want to show you kids up.

JASPER: That sounds like a challenge, Sue.

SUSAN: Are we talking how fast or how many? Because I already have a few years of drinking on you, don't you think? If we're counting lifetime totals, that is.

JASPER: Just a few years, though, Sue. A couple.

SUSAN: You didn't know me in my twenties, Jasper Taylor. There was a fair amount of drinking then.

JASPER: No, I didn't know you, Sue, but oh how I wish I did.

SUSAN: Well, if you're looking for a copy, check the girl across from you. (*pointing at Christina*) There's my mirror.

JASPER: Oh well, that isn't too bad, I guess.

CHRISTINA: Okay. So one for Dad. Here we go. One, two, three.

ALL except SUSAN shotgun a beer and chase with tequila.

NADINE: Yowza.

JASPER: Yip! Yip!

GORDON: Push me to shore.

SUSAN: It's nice to see everyone has a shared interest.

GORDON: Nadine.

GORDON takes NADINE over to the photos.

JASPER: Your hair.

CHRISTINA: What?

JASPER: You, uh –

CHRISTINA: What? Is it –

JASPER: No it, uh, you look nice today. Your hair does.

CHRISTINA: It does?

JASPER: It does.

CHRISTINA: I didn't really –

JASPER: I just thought you might like to know.

CHRISTINA: Thanks.

JASPER: Chris. You –

NADINE: Hey! Oh my god!

CHRISTINA: What?

NADINE: Guys, you have to come see this!

CHRISTINA: See what?

NADINE: Come here.

JASPER: What do you got there, kiddo?

   NADINE shows them a picture.

NADINE: Recognize anyone?

JASPER: Well, there's some good-looking people.

CHRISTINA: Holy crap.

NADINE: Is this from our first gig?

JASPER: Yup. That's Grand Bend, for sure. Hey, Chris?

CHRISTINA: Oh yeah.

JASPER: Look at us. My god. We had no idea how great we had it.

SUSAN: None of us do.

JASPER: What else you got in there, Gordo?

NADINE: Oh no!

CHRISTINA: There it is.

JASPER: Nadine, oh my god. I forgot you dyed your hair blue.

NADINE: It's not blue!

CHRISTINA: Purple. It's purple. She dyed it in that very bathroom.

NADINE: Don't remind me.

CHRISTINA: But you didn't have enough for the back, so it was party purple in the front ...

CHRISTINA and JASPER: ... and blond business in the back!

NADINE: Give me that! Well, at least I didn't have chicken legs, look at those babies.

CHRISTINA: Did I have chicken legs?

NADINE: Sticks in the sand.

JASPER: Well, if those are chicken legs, then cock-a-doodle-doo.

NADINE: Cluck-a-luck-luck.

JASPER: Do you – what's your plan for this stuff, Gordie?

> GORDON *makes a whooshing noise and pushes his hands out towards the lake.*

NADINE: What?

JASPER: All of it?

SUSAN: Gordon, you can't be serious. We just brought it all here. You're lucky it all didn't get eaten up in the tornado, for christ's sake.

CHRISTINA: He can do what he wants.

NADINE: But the memories.

JASPER: Do you have copies, Gordie?

GORDON: Just my paddle.

SUSAN: Not tonight, though, okay Gordon?

GORDON: When we're ready.

SUSAN: Nadine, you want to help me bring out some snacks from the kitchen?

NADINE: Me? Sure, Grandma.

SUSAN and NADINE exit.

CHRISTINA: Does she seem younger to you?

JASPER: Who?

CHRISTINA: Nadine.

GORDON: She's older.

CHRISTINA: Still a weirdo, though, still worrying all the time.

JASPER: You're all beautiful weirdos.

CHRISTINA: Are you feeling okay, Jasper?

JASPER: I'm feeling really good, actually.

CHRISTINA: Have you called your fiancée today?

JASPER: She called my mom earlier.

CHRISTINA: Okay.

JASPER: They like to talk to each other over Skype.

GORDON: Picture?

JASPER: Oh. Yeah. On my phone. Here we are mountain biking on real mountains in northern Iceland.

CHRISTINA: There's a northern Iceland? It's all pretty north already, isn't it?

JASPER: Chris, it's like a different planet. The landscape, well part of it, is volcanic rock. Dark chunks on top of each other. And hot springs.

CHRISTINA: Cool.

JASPER: And the music scene. They do whatever they want there and people go for it. It's like there's still a possibility for something new there, you know?

CHRISTINA: Right on.

JASPER: You'd like it there.

CHRISTINA: I think I like this planet. The one you're currently visiting.

JASPER: Well, you should consider coming to visit soon. I'll show you around.

CHRISTINA: Around Iceland.

GORDON: Look at the surfers.

JASPER: Oh yeah. It's good for that there, too.

GORDON: Catchin' waves.

JASPER: So many people spend the whole winter asleep and the summer surfing.

CHRISTINA: Iceland.

JASPER: Let's get you there, okay?

> SUSAN enters wearing a bathing suit. NADINE enters wearing a robe.

NADINE: Did anybody call for some snacks?

CHRISTINA: What?

NADINE: Because we got some hot, tasty bites right here.

JASPER: Whoa! Susan Marley. Looking good.

SUSAN: Oh yeah? Up for a swim?

JASPER: Always.

SUSAN: Well, we got a beach.

JASPER: I could even throw in a little water massage if you're feeling up for it.

SUSAN: Watch where you're pointing that charm, Jasper, or you might get what you ask for.

JASPER: Any time, any place, Sue. You know I love you Marley girls.

NADINE reveals that she is wearing one of her grandmother's bathing suits.

NADINE: Can I join in?

JASPER: Oh my god.

CHRISTINA: What the hell are you wearing?

NADINE: Like it?

JASPER: Those colours are out of this world.

CHRISTINA: Like a confused rocket.

NADINE: (*to CHRISTINA*) And I brought you out a little something I think you might like, too.

NADINE gives CHRISTINA an equally silly bathing suit.

CHRISTINA: I don't think so.

NADINE: Uh, come on.

CHRISTINA: Nah, Nadine –

NADINE: It would make me really happy.

CHRISTINA: You jerk, okay, gimme a minute.

CHRISTINA puts on the bathing suit over her clothes.

CHRISTINA: There. You happy?

NADINE: Aren't you? This is just wonderful.

CHRISTINA: (*to JASPER*) Don't you say a word.

JASPER: I'm scared to speak.

NADINE: Because you know you're getting one, too?

NADINE gives JASPER a silly bathing suit.

JASPER: Yes! Just what I always wanted.

JASPER puts on the bathing suit.

NADINE: Excellent!

CHRISTINA: Yowza!

SUSAN: Very nice.

NADINE: And Dad, this one's for you!

NADINE gives GORDON a bathing suit.

GORDON: Getting close to the water.

GORDON puts the bathing suit on his head.

NADINE: This might be the best thing that's ever happened to me.

CHRISTINA: Well, I'm sorry to hear that.

NADINE: I'm not. We look good.

JASPER: Well, I look good, anyway.

SUSAN: So, when do we get to meet the French boy, Nadine?

CHRISTINA: Tomorrow, right? We get to meet him tomorrow.

SUSAN: Good. It's about time.

JASPER: What's he like?

CHRISTINA: Would he put on one of Grandma's bathing suits with us?

JASPER: That's a good test.

CHRISTINA: Would he?

NADINE: Yeah. Well, I don't know. Probably.

SUSAN: You don't know?

NADINE: Well, yeah. I mean we haven't exactly been in this scenario before, so –

SUSAN: That's because he hasn't met the Marleys before!

CHRISTINA: But he would, though, wouldn't he?

NADINE: Sure. Yeah. Of course, but –

JASPER: Well, then he's my kind of guy.

SUSAN: Glad to hear it.

NADINE: But he –

SUSAN: Because I know it isn't easy finding the good people out there. The bad ones outnumber 'em, I'd say, so you really have to look.

NADINE: Does anybody …

CHRISTINA: What?

NADINE: Well, would you want to …

CHRISTINA: Have another tequila shot?

JASPER: Go for a late-night swim?

GORDON: Paddle and paddle and paddle and paddle.

NADINE: Does anybody want to go into town?

CHRISTINA: Right now?

JASPER: But you just got us all dressed up!

NADINE: I still haven't been yet.

CHRISTINA: It's late. What are you gonna do, clean in the dark?

SUSAN: Stick around and visit with your family, Nadine.

NADINE: Okay.

JASPER: I wrote a new song.

CHRISTINA: You did?

JASPER: Well, I've written a few, but I wrote this one for us. For Cottage Radio.

CHRISTINA: Can't we just rest in peace, already?

JASPER: I think you might like it.

SUSAN: I'm sure it's great.

NADINE: What's it about?

JASPER: It's a little dark, sort of.

GORDON: Play it.

NADINE: Yeah. I want to hear it.

JASPER: You might even ... well, it's pretty easy, so follow me and we can. Okay. Here.

JASPER plays the song "Freak King."

(*singing*) I thought you were already dead
Meant to forget myself instead
TV's on but you're not watching
Coffee table speaking Freak King, yeah
Man in the corner
Beer in throat
Tomorrow expires
Dark, black float.
You wear me down, update, update
Eating livers shaped like cupcakes
You go until you keep walking

Coffee table speaking Freak King, yeah
Girl in the corner
Earth in throat

NADINE joins JASPER singing.

Tomorrow expires
Dark, black float
Many sentences rapid-fire
Noting height on a tight wire
Landing home beeping calling

Coffee table speaking Freak King, yeah
Boy in corner
Hand in throat
Tomorrow expires
Dark, black float

Coffee table speaking Freak King, yeah
Coffee table speaking Freak King, yeah

NADINE goes big at the end of this song.

JASPER: Beauty. Nice one, Nadine.

NADINE: Thanks.

SUSAN: It's good, Jasper.

JASPER: Yeah, I think so too. I love it.

GORDON: Freak King, yeah.

JASPER: And you, Nadine, at the end there. You got it, I think. So much feeling.

CHRISTINA: Ehhh ...

NADINE: What?

CHRISTINA: Yes. Lots of feeling.

NADINE: But?

CHRISTINA: But nothing.

JASPER: No. Say it, but what?

CHRISTINA: Well, you guys know. I mean, it's a little self-indulgent.

JASPER: What? No way!

NADINE: Oh. Okay.

SUSAN: Christina!

CHRISTINA: I mean, in a very pretty way, but absolutely self-indulgent, come on. I love you guys, but it's just not us, obviously. Not Cottage Radio.

NADINE: Sure. Okay.

JASPER: Chris.

CHRISTINA: What? I'm not allowed to express my opinions?

NADINE: Of course you can.

JASPER: You can, but you're wrong, Chris.

NADINE: No. No. It's not wrong, it's –

JASPER: No. It is wrong and, well, kinda cold. Chris, you can be so cold sometimes.

SUSAN: Well, Jasper –

CHRISTINA: I don't even know why we're talking about this. We're not together anymore.

JASPER: What? Am I making you uncomfortable?

CHRISTINA: You're doing something.

SUSAN: I think it's good somebody's feeling something in this cottage.

JASPER: It probably felt pretty good, didn't it, kiddo?

NADINE: It did, but –

JASPER: Don't let her get to you, kiddo.

CHRISTINA: Look, yeah, of course it felt good for her. But will it feel good for everyone else? The audience?

JASPER: What?

CHRISTINA: Wouldn't it be better if we left the feeling to the audience and not ourselves?

JASPER: You don't want to feel anything when you make music?

NADINE: Chris is right.

JASPER: No. She's not. She's not always right.

NADINE: It's not worth it, Jasper.

JASPER: I think it's okay if a singer wants to indulge.

CHRISTINA: Well, I don't.

JASPER: Well, that's the end of it, then.

NADINE: Jasper.

JASPER: Yes.

NADINE: Where are we?

JASPER: What?

CHRISTINA: Yeah. Where are we?

JASPER: At your grandmother's cottage.

CHRISTINA: Exactly. Let's just – can we just stick to that?

NADINE: I'd really like to go into town.

CHRISTINA: Nadine, look at you. Stop. You're not going anywhere.

NADINE: You don't want to go into town?

CHRISTINA: Why should I?

NADINE: To –

CHRISTINA: Help out.

NADINE: Well, yeah.

GORDON: Help. Help. Help in the dark.

SUSAN: Nadine, it's late.

NADINE: Aren't you curious?

CHRISTINE: Help.

NADINE: Shouldn't we help?

CHRISTINA: I am helping.

NADINE: Chris?

CHRISTINA: What? Oh, no.

NADINE: What?

CHRISTINA: Please don't start.

NADINE: I didn't do anything.

CHRISTINA: Please just don't.

NADINE: Don't what?

CHRISTINA: I just don't want you to. Just stop. Don't get into it
    with me, just don't.

NADINE: I didn't do anything.

JASPER: She didn't do anything, Chris.

CHRISTINA: Just stop. Don't pretend like you weren't
    just about to –

NADINE: What? What am I about to do?

CHRISTINA: To do this. You know. Don't. You fucking know.

NADINE: What do I know?

JASPER: What does she know?

CHRISTINA: You shit. You're about to launch into a million questions, a thousand fucking questions about who I am and what I'm doing with my life. Interrogate me.

NADINE: Interrogate? I'm not.

CHRISTINA: In front of everyone.

JASPER: Chris.

CHRISTINA: You are.

NADINE: I'm not.

CHRISTINA: You fucking were. Don't pretend that you weren't.

NADINE: Well, Chris –

CHRISTINA: Here we go!

NADINE: Chris.

CHRISTINA: Stop. Just stop.

NADINE: Chris.

CHRISTINA: I'm begging. Literally begging you to stop.

NADINE: I need to talk, people need to talk.

CHRISTINA: No, they don't. They really don't.

NADINE: Don't you want to talk?

CHRISTINA: Nobody has got to do anything. Nothing. Anything.

NADINE: Chris.

CHRISTINA: What?

NADINE: Will you please come to town with me and see
it and see –

CHRISTINA: No! I don't want to leave. You can't make me leave.

NADINE: You don't know what you're missing.

SUSAN: Now, Nadine.

NADINE: It's all out there, the world.

CHRISTINA: You swoop in from outer space and you think you
can fix me? I don't need fixing.

JASPER: Chris, are you okay?

NADINE: We all have to talk sometimes. I want to talk
about things.

SUSAN: Nadine, that's –

NADINE: I'm home for, what, twenty-four hours and I'm already
tired of it. Aren't you guys getting tired of it?

CHRISTINA: She's tired of it.

JASPER: Nadine, maybe you should –

NADINE: No. I'm right, Jasper. Jasper, don't you think we should
talk about things, sometimes?

JASPER: Nadine, I don't know what you want me to say here.

NADINE: See. He can't. He can't anymore, either. It's been so long and Grandma –

CHRISTINA: Nadine.

NADINE: And Grandma here, poor fucking Grandma, always picking up after her own granddaughter.

SUSAN: That's not –

NADINE: Her thirty-year-old granddaughter. The one with all the promise. So funny. So cool. Grandma's still waiting for you to blossom. How sad is that?

JASPER: Nadine.

NADINE: It's sad.

SUSAN: I think that's enough.

NADINE: I don't. I hate that I'm here right now. That you all are there and I'm here. This isn't my cottage anymore, and I hate it. It looks the same, but it's not. Not to me. I've changed.

SUSAN: You're exactly the same.

NADINE: No, I'm not.

SUSAN: You're out there, handling everything on your own. There's no need to come home and gang up on Christina –

NADINE: Gang up on Christina? I am ganging up on her? Now that's funny.

SUSAN: Stop. Like a good girl.

NADINE: Like a good girl. Well, I'm not a good girl.

SUSAN: You are.

NADINE: I'm not. I thought I was, but I'm failing at it, Grandma. You think so yourself. Don't even pretend. I can't even be a strong Marley girl. I'm another stupid, typical girl who makes mistakes and trusts too much and fails. I'm failing. You know what? I called François today, and he offered to come down early. Come down today.

SUSAN: Well, that's great. I'm excited to meet him.

NADINE: Well, I don't want him to meet you. I told him no, don't come, and that I would leave early tomorrow to come back. Chris will say one thing to the guy, and I might as well go shopping for a new French boy, 'cause that guy won't want to be a part of this. This mess. I hate this. I thought I knew what I was doing. It looks so easy being happy, but it's not, not coming from this. And soon I have to go back –

CHRISTINA: You don't have to go back. You can stay here with me, kiddo, and I'll take care of you.

NADINE: You want me to come here and take care of me?

CHRISTINA: Yeah. You can come stay for a while.

JASPER: Chris.

SUSAN: No. She can't stay here.

CHRISTINA: No? Just no, Grandma?

SUSAN: She can't.

JASPER: She's got a life and an apartment and friends in Toronto. She's gotta figure it out, Chris.

SUSAN: She can't stay here. There's no more rotting in this cottage allowed. You can't stay here.

GORDON: Chris.

CHRISTINA: What?

GORDON: Tell her how you speak to her.

NADINE: What?

GORDON: Every day. Over the radio.

CHRISTINA: No.

GORDON: Who's your audience, Chris?

CHRISTINA: Please.

GORDON: It's all for her. She prepares it all so she would like it. The whole radio show.

CHRISTINA: Stop.

GORDON: She thinks about what she'd get a kick out of and says that.

SUSAN: She sure does.

GORDON: She's a good girl, eh, Sue? Christina's a good girl talking to her all the time.

SUSAN: She's a good girl talking to her all the time.

> GORDON brings over a photo album from the raft. NADINE looks at a photo of her mother.

NADINE: What's it like talking to her all the time?

CHRISTINA: I don't know.

NADINE: You don't know?

CHRISTINA: I don't know.

NADINE: Why can't you just – what's it like, can't you tell me?

CHRISTINA: I don't know, I –

NADINE: Holy shit. I need to know. Why can't you just tell me? I need to know.

GORDON: She likes it.

JASPER: No, Gordon. She has to say it.

NADINE: Say it. Tell me.

CHRISTINA: It's not easy.

NADINE: Nothing is easy. It's not easy to admit I miss her, but there, I miss her. Now you.

CHRISTINA: Nadine. I, I –

NADINE: Okay. How about you admit something else, then? How about you admit you want Jasper to stay? That you want Jasper not to return to Iceland and not to marry the Icelandic beauty and to stay here instead and marry you. Will you admit that?

CHRISTINA: You can't just –

NADINE: You *can* just. You can open up your mouth and just say it.

JASPER: She doesn't, though.

NADINE: Oh, she does.

SUSAN: Jasper, your future.

JASPER: She doesn't want me.

CHRISTINA: You haven't asked.

JASPER: I have. I did.

CHRISTINA: Not the way you should have and you know it. You don't want me. You think you do, but you don't. Not really. You want Iceland.

JASPER: What kind of bullshit is that? You know what, I would give it all up for you and you know I would do all that for you and you would let me and let me be miserable, because you don't even want me back.

SUSAN: Have you even asked her?

NADINE: No. I think it's up to Chris for once.

SUSAN: Have you asked her, Jasper?

JASPER: She won't say yes.

NADINE: Exactly. She needs to admit she wants to.

SUSAN: She's right there.

CHRISTINA: Grandma.

SUSAN: Ask her, if you want to ask her.

NADINE: Admit it, Chris.

JASPER: Chris, I –

CHRISTINA: Jasper.

JASPER: But I –

CHRISTINA: No. Don't worry about it.

NADINE: See.

SUSAN: You haven't asked. Really asked.

JASPER: I –

CHRISTINA: No. Okay. It's not very fun to have you coerced into asking me here. It's okay.

JASPER: But Chris, I –

CHRISTINA: Feel pressured. Yeah, I know. Well, here. Don't waste your time. See, it's actually an easy situation for him, because no part of me wants to go. No. Okay. No.

JASPER: No part of you?

CHRISTINA: No. I told you I like it here.

NADINE: Chris.

CHRISTINA: It's better off this way, trust me. You know me, don't you think I know me? It's okay.

SUSAN: Christina, if you just let him ask, then you –

CHRISTINA: Nope. Go, Jasper. Leave.

NADINE: You don't have to leave.

JASPER: I'm sorry.

CHRISTINA: You're sorry? Go.

JASPER: I –

CHRISTINA: I tried.

> *JASPER exits.*

CHRISTINA: Oh, that must have been fun for you, you all.

SUSAN: What?

CHRISTINA: Especially you, Nadine. So fun making my life even shittier than it was before. Give me back that picture.

NADINE: What?

CHRISTINA: Well, you got what you wanted, I guess. A cry buddy. We can look at the sad tornado things together tomorrow and cry.

NADINE: That's not fair. I admitted I'm not happy. That was not easy to do.

CHRISTINA: You made me disappoint Grandma.

SUSAN: No, I –

CHRISTINA: And you're embarrassed of me anyway, right? Couldn't bring your French boy to meet me, because you're scared he'll see you differently after meeting me.

NADINE: Yup.

CHRISTINA: And you're making me be a stupid girl just like you. Good work. Excellent job. Thank you.

NADINE: You're welcome.

CHRISTINA: This is all your fault.

SUSAN: Girls.

CHRISTINA: You're turning into Mom.

NADINE: I'm turning into Mom? Me?

CHRISTINA: That's what I said.

NADINE: And that's all I can handle. You want to be alone, you want to drive us all away again, well good work, because I'm headed for the door.

CHRISTINA: Fantastic.

NADINE: The cottage is all yours, you can hang out with your future over there and worry Grandma some more until we don't have her to worry anymore.

CHRISTINA: Yup. Perfect.

SUSAN: Girls! Listen to yourselves.

NADINE: And keep on with your stupid dead-end radio show that nobody even listens to or cares about and the only time it was ever useful to Goderich you wouldn't let people call in and say thank you for being alive. Great work.

CHRISTINA: Get the hell out, Nadine.

NADINE: Gladly.

SUSAN: Girls!

NADINE: Hope you can find enough booze around here to help you out of this one.

NADINE exits to the beach with a blanket.

ACT 3, SCENE 4
FREAK KING

GORDON does a solo verse of "Freak King."

GORDON:
  (*singing*) I thought you were already dead
  Meant to forget myself instead
  TV's on but you're not watching

  Coffee table speaking Freak King, yeah
  Man in the corner
  Beer in throat
  Tomorrow expires
  Dark, black float
  You wear me down, update, update
  Eating livers shaped like cupcakes
  You go until you keep walking

  Coffee table speaking Freak King, yeah
  Coffee table speaking Freak King, yeah

ACT 3, SCENE 5
PADDLE HOME

The following morning. CHRISTINA is alone on the couch. GORDON is on the deck.

CHRISTINA: Ehhhh …

SUSAN: I'm just off for my swim now, Christina. You start your radio show in a few minutes.

CHRISTINA: Not today.

SUSAN: Yes, today. Let's go, Christina. You want to go for a quick dip first with me in the lake? Wake up?

CHRISTINA: No thanks.

SUSAN: Well, you aren't going to disappoint your listeners.

CHRISTINA: Do you mind if I interview you?

SUSAN: Now?

CHRISTINA: On the radio.

CHRISTINA sets up the radio show and sits down with SUSAN.

CHRISTINA: Hello, Goderich, and welcome back to the *Cottage Radio* show with Chris. And we wrestled the sexy Sue Marley from the lake. Welcome, Grandma.

SUSAN: I love being welcomed into my own living room.

CHRISTINA: You know, I think most of my ratings actually come from people waiting to hear you on the show, Grandma.

SUSAN: I doubt that very much.

CHRISTINA: I'm pretty sure.

SUSAN: Christina, that can't be true, with all your loyal fans.

CHRISTINA: Loyal. How long have you had this cottage, Grandma?

SUSAN: Oh, since your grandfather bought it, I suppose. A short while before your mother was born.

CHRISTINA: You used to bring her out here a lot?

SUSAN: Oh, she loved it here. Loved to swim, paddle, kick, dive, float. Nadine was like that, too.

CHRISTINA: Not me?

SUSAN: You were your own in the water.

CHRISTINA: What do you mean, Grandma?

SUSAN: Your love for water was different. It was hard to keep you from walking out into it, but you always sank like a little stone. You have a caller, Christina.

CHRISTINA: I see that.

SUSAN: Are you planning on taking it?

CHRISTINA: I ... okay. Hello, *Cottage Radio.*

RHONDA: Hello.

RALPH: Hi there.

CHRISTINA: Would you, uh, do you have a story to share?

RHONDA: My mom has a small place.

RALPH: Off highway twenty-one, just south of town.

RHONDA: Pretty close to the water.

CHRISTINA: Oh yeah?

RHONDA: So we spend a lot of time in Goderich during the summer.

RALPH: Our wedding, even.

RHONDA: We got married thirteen years ago, now.

RALPH: On one of those beauty summer days.

RHONDA: Gorgeous.

CHRISTINA: A little difference weather from last Sunday?

RALPH: No, no.

RHONDA: Yeah.

RALPH: Not the same at all.

   SUSAN exits to the beach.

RHONDA: Last weekend, Mom asked us down.

RALPH: Like usual.

RHONDA: And Sunday we ended up in town.

RALPH: At Zellers.

RHONDA: Then on the square a bit.

RALPH: And headed into Zehrs for dinner supplies on
the way back.

RHONDA: Remember those clouds, the way they looked
on the way in?

RALPH: Oh yeah. Furious.

RHONDA: Dark.

RALPH: Inside, we heard it then.

RHONDA: A whoosh.

RALPH: And a crack!

RHONDA: I ran us over to the first checkout counter.

RALPH: Like we were robbing the place.

RHONDA: I thought about my mom then, hoping she was away
from her windows.

RALPH: There was lightning like mad, and the hydro went out.

RHONDA: I mean, it didn't last long.

RALPH: Thirty seconds tops. A minute.

RHONDA: Outside it looked messy and the kid with the carts
looked confused.

RALPH: I ran over to him and he was stunned but fine.

RHONDA: He told me he almost got hit in the head with the cart
he was trying to put in the stack with the others.

RALPH: In shock, for sure.

RHONDA: He just stood there staring at that cart like it was wild and decided to fly up and bite him on its own.

RALPH: Like he did something to it and the cart got mad.

RHONDA: I explained it was a tornado.

RALPH: But he didn't look very convinced.

RHONDA: No.

CHRISTINA: Well, thank you for your story ...

RALPH: Ralph.

RHONDA: And Rhonda.

CHRISTINA: Thank you, Ralph, and thank you, Rhonda, for calling in and making sure we all know you're still alive.

RALPH: Any time.

CHRISTINA: And I guess I should thank you, you all, for calling in at all, letting me in on your stories of what the storm has done to your houses, your front lawns, your porches, your businesses. And how it touched your life and the lives of your brothers, your moms, your daughters, your partners. Because this radio station is for you, not for me, like I sometimes think. It's for you.

I'm realizing now that you did the same for me. You listened, too. You listened to me when I needed it most, when I missed her the most, my wild woman of a mother. She was really something, but I'm sure I don't need to tell you that. She was likely your favourite person, and maybe your least favourite person too. I'm sure you had an opinion about her, anyway, and you were patient with me, letting me talk, letting me grieve over the airwaves in my weird way. Thank you.

I guess the least I can do now is let you call in and just say your piece. Don't worry. I won't stop you anymore. Call away! But I will say that I couldn't help but notice that my name was not mentioned on any of your thank-you lists. Not one. I didn't make the cut. Nobody.

SUSAN enters from the lake and sits on the deck with GORDON.

But what have you done, Christina? Besides stopping you from telling you your stories, I have sat here and had some beers and felt sorry for myself and talked to my sister and my dad and my grandmother and Jasper. I've been trying to act normal when it was basically impossible and got angry that it was so hard. That doesn't make a thank-you list, and I think I'm starting to get why.

Okay. And we have another caller. Hello, Cottage Radio.

GORDON: (*calling in from the deck*) When the power went out, I was already holding a section of our wall in my hands.

CHRISTINA: Dad?

GORDON: I hear how everyone ran for cover in their basements and that does seem like a logical course of action to partake in but I – well, logic's never been my way. The sound that came first like a, an aircraft hitting my roof pushed me to the attic. So by the time I got up there, I was back down again on the ground floor. The beams rushing in on themselves. Twisting. Crushing. I lied there for a while and the aircraft sound stayed in my ears long enough I wasn't sure if I was yelling out or keeping quiet. The attic's where all her things were, blasted on the floor. The house beside ours still standing. The kids came out of it pointing at me, giving me enough strength to pull myself out of it. I didn't want to leave, but I needed to go out to the water, so I found my paddle and an inflatable boat from the front room. A young guy in his underwear directing traffic, so I thought I should follow where he told me to go. And I did for a while. Walking alongside others. Some doing good. Some encouraging the good, you know. And something about a gas leak, so I was left alone on the road. For the most part, I tried to heal things on the way to the water. Myself and others and trees. A woman let me hold a brick from her house in my hands and give respects. I buried it later. In those situations you really think you're helping. You're there seeing and holding, so you think that'll lead to healing, but what's healing? Restoring it? Putting it back together? Making something new? That woman will never be able to find her brick now. And in all my years living in this place, I've never paddled along the beach like that. I got to the shore and blew up the inflatable raft. I got in and paddled all the way here, to you, Chris. The roads shouldn't have to be closed for us to paddle home.

JASPER: (*over the radio*) Chris.

CHRISTINA: Jasper?

JASPER: I'm sorry I didn't ask you.

CHRISTINA: Ask me what?

JASPER: If you wanted to go to Iceland.

CHRISTINA: But I told you a long time ago I didn't want to go.

JASPER: I know. I shouldn't have asked then, that day.

CHRISTINA: Are you leaving?

JASPER: Will you come with me?

CHRISTINA: To Iceland? No fucking way.

JASPER: Or somewhere else.

CHRISTINA: But you –

JASPER: Chris. Please. Let me take you somewhere.

CHRISTINA: I think you might have some conversations that need having first, Jasper.

JASPER: Conversations?

CHRISTINA: In Iceland, I mean.

JASPER: Uh, yeah.

CHRISTINA: You should go have them first, those conversations.

JASPER: They might not be fun conversations.

CHRISTINA: They will definitely not be fun, no.

JASPER: And after those conversations are done?

CHRISTINA: You'll come home, okay?

JASPER: Okay.

CHRISTINA: Okay.

JASPER: You, Christina Marley, are admitting that you want me to come home over the radio?

CHRISTINA: Those words came out of my mouth.

JASPER: Do you? Tell me you want me to come home, Chris.

    NADINE enters.

CHRISTINA: After those conversations, Jasper, and only after them, I want you to – well, I mean, actually maybe – I, I don't know, fuck, there's just a lot of people involved in this and I –

NADINE: You were so close.

CHRISTINA: Jasper.

JASPER: Yeah.

CHRISTINA: Nose to eye socket.

JASPER: Whatever you say.

CHRISTINA: Hi Nadine.

NADINE: I think I'm ready.

CHRISTINA: Did you go to town?

NADINE: Yup. Are you ready, Dad?

GORDON: Ready.

NADINE: Grandma?

SUSAN: Ready.

NADINE: Are you ready, Chris?

CHRISTINA: Yeah.

NADINE: Can I make a request?

CHRISTINA: Anything you like.

NADINE: How about a little a cappella version of "Salt."

CHRISTINA: You got it. Here it comes, Goderich.

> CHRISTINA straps the microphone to her body. As they sing
> "Salt," CHRISTINA and NADINE walk out to the deck and
> with the help of SUSAN and GORDON take the raft with the
> photos of Mom out to the water.

CHRISTINA and **NADINE:**
(*singing*) Did you want to tell me why
You look for me in the sky
When below the water
Sits my mother
And my bitter-tasting lullaby?

Who didn't tell you
We've already been through
The most of this
The truth of this
Eyes off the skies?

Dig holes under the lake
With metal forks and plates
In search of me
Getaway spree.

Sunk hard like I was salt.
Sunk hard like I was salt.

Blackout.

The End

White Wedding

Left to right: Jeanette Dagger, Lauren Wolanski, Kayla Whelan, Dave Martin, and Cass Van Wyck in *White Wedding* at Artscape Youngplace, July 2017

Photograph by Eilish Waller

PRODUCTION HISTORY

White Wedding was first produced from July 5 to 16, 2017, at Artscape Youngplace in Toronto, Ontario, with the following cast and crew: .

LISA:	Kayla Whelan
JASON:	Nabil Traboulsi
HEATHER:	Cass Van Wyck
GABRIELLE:	Ermina Pérez
DAVE:	Dave Martin
MARGOT:	Jeanette Dagger
CARL:	Daniel Cristofori
MICHELLE:	Lauren Wolanski
ANNIE:	Abby Weisbrot
Director:	Taylor Marie Graham
Assistant Directors and Stage Managers:	Sebastian Biasucci and Emily Jenkins
Set and Costume Designer:	Lindsay Woods
Music Arranger:	Dave Martin

CHARACTERS

LISA: Twenty-three to thirty-five-ish (*same age as Jason, Carl, Heather, and Michelle*), Ph.D. candidate, in a relationship with a famous author, Carl's best friend, great friends with Heather, Michelle, and Jason, intimidated by Margot, thinks of Dave as an uncle.

JASON: Twenty-three to thirty-five-ish (*same age as Lisa, Carl, Heather, and Michelle*), an artist, takes his art very seriously, married to Michelle, great friends with Carl and Dave, has a young child, known as J.

GABRIELLE: Two or three years younger than Lisa and co., came to Canada as a child, Carl's bride, went to school with Lisa, Heather, Michelle, and Jason.

HEATHER: Twenty-three to thirty-five-ish (*same age as Jason, Carl, Lisa, and Michelle*), sarcastic, in love and in a sexual relationship with Michelle, great friends with Lisa and Dave.

MICHELLE: Twenty-three to thirty-five-ish (*same age as Jason, Carl, Heather, and Lisa*), Carl's twin sister, married to J, has a young child, in a sexual relationship with Heather, quick to anger, Margot's granddaughter.

CARL: Twenty-three to thirty-five-ish (*same age as Jason, Carl, Heather, and Michelle*), lovable, friendly, and sarcastic, a lawyer, Lisa's best friend and ex-lover, Gabrielle's groom, Michelle's twin brother, Margot's grandson.

DAVE: Least three years older than Lisa and co., a great guitar player, a small-time drug dealer, caring, genuine, has a fun sense of humour.

MARGOT: Sixty-five plus, perceptive, sarcastic, Carl and Michelle's grandmother.

ANNIE: Any age, photographer.

SETTING

The play takes place at a recently renovated high school that has embraced modernism. The action is on the second-floor hallway which now looks more like an art gallery than a high school. There are classroom doors and a pair of washrooms, as well as doors which lead to downstairs.

Below, on the first floor, a wedding reception is about to take place. The bride and groom both went to this high school, and that's why their wedding is happening here. Throughout the play, as doors open music and sound travels into the space from downstairs.

TIME

This play was originally set in 2017; however new creative teams are welcome to change the time period. It is summer.

SCENE 1
WEDDING SONG

As the audience enters, JASON is creating an art project as a gift for the bride with the help of DAVE. The key theme for the art project is "snow machine." DAVE plays his pared-back version of a traditionally popular wedding song (something like "Y.M.C.A.") on the guitar as JASON fusses with his art project.

JASON: (*cutting off the song at a key point*) No, no. Not that one.

DAVE plays his version of another popular wedding song on the guitar. This could be something currently popular.

JASON: (*cutting off the song at a key point*) Nope. Try again.

DAVE plays his version of "White Wedding" or another wedding song that will be reprised later. JASON gets into it.

JASON: (*cutting off the song at a key point*) Yes. That will do.

MARGOT enters.

MARGOT: Okay, boys, they're coming!

MARGOT exits.

JASON and DAVE quickly cover their art-project-in-process with a sheet and exit into the boy's washroom carrying one of the bigger pieces to hide it.

SCENE 2
SKULL

CARL, GABRIELLE, and ANNIE enter.

ANNIE: Okay. So this is where I'm going to take the last few shots and then I'll return you to your guests. I like the light in here right now.

CARL: Where do you want us?

ANNIE: First maybe hold her hand. Yeah, like that, good. And walk that way.

CARL and GABRIELLE start walking.

ANNIE: Perfect. Slowly.

CARL: I bet I can walk slower than you can. Slow-walk competition?

GABRIELLE: I think we should probably walk as slow as each other, otherwise the photos might come out kinda weird.

CARL: Sure ... everything okay over there?

GABRIELLE: Of course.

CARL: You seem a little ...

GABRIELLE: What?

CARL: Maybe this is a bit of a stretch, but I thought you'd look happier on our wedding day.

ANNIE: Stop!

CARL and GABRIELLE stop walking.

ANNIE: Good. Now face each other.

CARL and GABRIELLE face each other and drop hands.

ANNIE: No, keep holding hands.

CARL and GABRIELLE hold hands.

ANNIE: A little higher. There.

GABRIELLE: I am happy.

CARL: I've seen you happy. You don't look happy.

GABRIELLE: You know I don't like to smile in pictures.

CARL: Even on the happiest day of your life?

ANNIE: And now a dip please.

CARL and GABRIELLE dip awkwardly.

CARL: Is it the venue?

GABRIELLE: No! I love being here where we met in our stupid uniforms.

CARL: Do you wish you were still in our school uniforms? Because I think I still have mine at my grandma's place somewhere. And I'm not going to lie, I wouldn't mind seeing you in your kilt again.

GABRIELLE: Wedding dress isn't doing it for ya?

CARL: You are doing it for me, full stop on that one. Wedding dress helps, though, yeah. Nice bead work? I don't know how to compliment a wedding dress, I'm sorry.

GABRIELLE: It's the weather, Carl. I thought I would get over a winter wedding, but I really do miss the snow. Especially for the pictures, you know?

CARL: Oh.

ANNIE: Dip lower, please.

CARL and GABRIELLE try to dip lower.

GABRIELLE: I'm sorry. I didn't think I'd still feel this way.

CARL: It's hard to get people here in the snow, Gabs.

GABRIELLE: I know.

CARL: But you still miss it.

GABRIELLE: Weddings. Snow lightly falling. It's just always made so much sense to me.

ANNIE: Relax for just one second.

CARL and GABRIELLE stand up as ANNIE looks through some of the pictures.

GABRIELLE: Ever since my family immigrated here in the dead of winter when I was eight, the snow was so romantic to me, you know? Exotic. We got out of the cab and there was no wind and I knew the snow was cold, but it actually looked warm to me, like wool on everything. I remember being so nervous coming here, like I didn't know if I would have anyone to talk to, but the snow comforted me, it was so beautiful and reliable. I expected it to come every winter, and it always did.

ANNIE: And now can you pick her up?

CARL picks GABRIELLE up.

CARL: Well, we could always have another one.

GABRIELLE: Another wedding? To each other, you mean?

CARL: Sure. Why not? Who says we have to make it a once-in-a-lifetime event? We could make it annual, biannual even, if you really wanted. We could do a summer and a winter wedding every year.

GABRIELLE: You would want to marry me that many times?

CARL: Well, we marry each other every morning we decide not to run off to Antarctica or Sweden or wherever, don't we? Why not celebrate that a few times a year?

ANNIE: I'm almost done with you. It's time to pucker up. To sha-la-la-la, kiss the girl.

CARL and GABRIELLE kiss. LISA enters carrying a gift.

LISA: Oh shit. Sorry.

CARL: Lisa?

LISA: I'm so sorry. I thought everything was happening up here, but I shouldn't be up here.

CARL puts GABRIELLE down, runs over to LISA, and picks her up in a big swinging circle.

CARL: Lisa! I'm so glad you're here! You just arrived, didn't you?

LISA: No?

CARL: You did. You're late to my wedding.

LISA: I know, I'm sorry. I –

CARL: And where's your cool, older, famous-writer guy?

LISA: He couldn't make it.

CARL: You're late and you didn't bring someone famous to my wedding? Why did you even come?

LISA: I'm so sorry, Carl, I –

CARL: You are not forgiven.

LISA: I'm not?

CARL: Say sorry to my wife.

LISA: Oh my god. Hey, Gabrielle.

GABRIELLE: Hi.

LISA: I'm sorry for being late to your wedding. I bet it was very pretty.

CARL: It was, and now me.

LISA: I'm so sorry, really Carl, I'm a shit of a person.

CARL: Yes, you are, but that thing in your hand there might help me forgive ya.

LISA: Oh yeah. I brought you a present.

CARL: You sure did.

LISA: Do you want it now?

CARL: It's for me, isn't it?

LISA: Yes! Well, for the plural you, I guess. Yous.

> LISA gives GABRIELLE the gift.

GABRIELLE: Thank you.

CARL: I'm opening it.

GABRIELLE: Carl.

CARL: This better be good.

CARL opens the present. There's a skull inside.

LISA: It's nothing, really. I just saw it when I was travelling in Peru last summer and I remember how you used to like skulls. Do you still like skulls?

CARL: I love it. Isn't it awesome, Gabs?

GABRIELLE: It's very thoughtful.

CARL: I haven't seen you since last summer?

LISA: Christmas, actually. Two Christmases ago. I haven't been home at all since then.

ANNIE: Excuse me –

CARL: And you still arrived late to my wedding.

LISA: With a skull. For you.

ANNIE: I think it's time to –

CARL: It's a pretty super-sweet wedding present. I'll give you that.

GABRIELLE: Carl.

CARL: Yes, my bride?

GABRIELLE: I think maybe we have to –

CARL: Oh man. We gotta head downstairs.

GABRIELLE: Yeah.

LISA: Oh okay. Lead the way!

GABRIELLE: Well, actually ...

CARL: Oh. Yeah. You can't come with us downstairs, Leese.

LISA: No? Sure. Yeah, no problem.

CARL: Yeah, it would be weird if all three of us arrived at the reception together!

GABRIELLE: We practised an entrance.

LISA: Oh.

CARL: It's very cool. I get to twirl. And she gets to twirl.

LISA: No problem. I'll hang back a bit.

GABRIELLE: And the, uh, bones?

CARL: Oh, Lisa can babysit this for a while longer, can't you, Leese?

LISA: Not a problem.

CARL: Cool, thanks. See you down there.

> CARL, LISA, and ANNIE start to exit. LISA runs and yells after them.

LISA: Hey, Carl!

CARL: Yeah, Leese?

LISA: Congratulations!

SCENE 3
NIAGARA FALLS

As LISA looks down the stairs, a song like The Frank and Walters' version of "After All" starts playing from downstairs for CARL and GABRIELLE's entrance.

VOICEOVER: And here we go, everyone. May I present the bride and groom, Mr. and Mrs. Burk!

Cheers from downstairs. LISA starts to panic a little and begins crying.

LISA: Oh. Oh no. No, no, no, no. Not again. Stop. Please stop. Okay. I'm okay.

DAVE and JASON enter from the washroom. LISA hides her face and tears. DAVE and JASON continue setting up the snow-machine art project throughout the following scene. It's evolving and changing as the scene progresses.

JASON: Now, this is what I was thinking we'd try next. I don't know if I have enough extension cords at this time.

DAVE: Oh hey, look, it's little Lisa.

JASON: (*holding up part of the snow machine*) Hey Lisa, does this look like a corn chip or a snowflake to you?

LISA finally turns to face them.

LISA: Hi you guys, what were you doing in there?

DAVE: Planning the earth's total destruction.

LISA: With nachos?

JASON: I knew it looked too much like a corn chip.

DAVE: Corn chips could do a lot of damage under the right circumstances.

JASON: But damage isn't what we're going for here. It might look like a mess right now, but in a few hours, this floor will outdo the beauty of the Taj Mahal, Niagara Falls –

DAVE: Niagara Falls? Canada's national treasure? I don't know if we're gonna top that, my friend.

LISA: Oh. This is an art project! I missed these.

JASON: I didn't know you had such a fondness for Niagara Falls.

DAVE: Have you seen Niagara Falls lately? I went there two weeks ago because I was asked to play a few tunes at this dingy club on the outskirts, but I decided to go in down Clifton Hill, past all the Vegas-inspired haunted houses and celebrity wax museums, to see the falls themselves, because I hadn't really, since I was younger than you folk. And there was this Irish family there. I was watching them watch the falls, and it was one of those moments, you know. Real awe all over their faces. I didn't realize how much I take the wonder of this pretty blue planet for granted. That's real beauty.

JASON: Yeah, well we're gonna top it today.

DAVE: If you say so.

LISA: What's the plan?

JASON: This one's commissioned by the groom himself.

LISA: Carl, you mean?

JASON: He will have high expectations.

DAVE: It's gonna be good, little Lisa. I think J's got a nice vision on this one.

JASON: It will be my best work.

LISA: Can I help?

JASON: I might have a role for you to play. Can you grab that for me?

> *JASON instructs LISA to grab something electrical, which is hot.*

LISA: Ow!

JASON: Oh, was that hot?

DAVE: Lisa, are you okay?

> *DAVE notices for the first time that LISA has been crying.*

J, I think you made her cry.

LISA: No, no. I'm not crying.

DAVE: But you –

LISA: Not crying. I'm completely fine.

JASON: Should I fetch some cold water for your hand?

LISA: I'm good. All good.

DAVE: Here.

> *DAVE takes ice out of the snow machine and a little towel. He gently wraps LISA's hand.*

LISA: Thank you ...

JASON: I will, of course, do a project for your wedding to the famous writer should you wish, Lisa. Pro bono. My rate is getting very high these days, but for you, nothing.

LISA: That's very nice.

JASON: Is he downstairs? I was hoping I could bounce a couple script ideas off him. I always thought I would end up writing major motion pictures.

LISA: He's not downstairs.

JASON: Where is he? My ideas are very good.

DAVE: J.

LISA: You'll have to catch him next time.

JASON: Oh. I see.

LISA: J, I remember the gorgeous art project you put together for Michelle at your wedding.

JASON: Yeah, I regret not going bigger with that one.

LISA: She loved it.

JASON: But did it blow her to pieces?

LISA: I don't know.

   MARGOT enters with a drink and some supplies for JASON.

MARGOT: I remember that day too, you know, J. My lawn was covered in glitter and popsicle sticks for weeks.

JASON: Your backyard was the ideal place for a project such as this in terms of time and scheduling, Margot. I was lucky to be able to try out various versions of my plan months in advance.

MARGOT: I remember. Again, my lawn has never been the same.

JASON: The end result was very calculable, unlike this venture, as I am expected to pull off this feat today. I can't believe I didn't have access to the space beforehand.

MARGOT: Well, lucky for you this is your old high school then, eh? You'll figure it out. So long as you don't drop all this junk off on my lawn later, I'll be happy. I think there's another washroom up here, so I thought I would –

LISA: Hey, Margot.

MARGOT: Hi, Lisa girl. Are you okay?

LISA: Yes.

MARGOT: Are you sure?

LISA: Perfectly fine.

MARGOT: Okay. Look I really have to, so you don't mind if I –

LISA: No. No. Do your thing.

MARGOT: Can I get you to hold this for me?

LISA: Sure.

> MARGOT *gives* LISA *her drink and goes into the washroom.*
> *She surprises* LISA *by yelling out to her from the stall.*
> JASON *and* DAVE *continue to set up the machine.*

MARGOT: Can you believe our Carl actually got married?

LISA: No! Well, I mean, yes of course, but no!

MARGOT: As you know, that girl he nabbed is much too good for him, but I won't tell her if you don't!

LISA: Yeah.

MARGOT: Did you know they originally wanted to have a winter wedding?

LISA: No.

MARGOT: Who decides to have a winter wedding? I mean, Jesus. Only my idiot grandson could think it was romantic or something, eh Lisa?

LISA: Sounds like Carl.

MARGOT: I'm glad I could talk him out of it! I mean, it would have been cheap. I'm not an idiot, it would be so much cheaper than Michelle's big princess wedding that my ruined lawn five years ago, but that's no way to think of a wedding. Money.

LISA: It must be strange for you now that both Michelle and Carl are married?

The sound of a toilet flushing and sink water flowing. MARGOT enters from the washroom.

MARGOT: It's moments like this that you feel very old, Lisa girl.

LISA: You look young to me.

MARGOT: Very funny. They turned out okay, though, didn't they? They can both be kind of little monsters sometimes, especially Michelle, my god. But at least they're good-looking, though, am I right?

LISA: Very good-looking.

MARGOT: My beauty twin grandbabies all married up. And with babies of their own now. By the way, J, did you know your child is making the rounds untethered downstairs?

JASON: Michelle's not downstairs? She knows I have work to do.

LISA: Wait, J, did you and Michelle have a baby?

JASON: Of course. My boy Leo.

LISA: Baby Leo.

JASON: Margot, I specifically said I was doing work, so Michelle should know this is where I am.

LISA: How did I not hear about this? Michelle and J have a baby.

MARGOT: Michelle's posted a thousand photos on Facebook. And I bet a bunch of people downstairs are doing the same right now.

DAVE: Lisa's not into Facebook. She's more free than that.

LISA: I don't like Facebook, no. I feel it cheapens real-life moments.

DAVE: Right on, Lisa girl. Baby Leo's a cute little snapper, though.

MARGOT: He looks exactly like my Michelle.

DAVE: But acts like this guy, if you can believe it.

JASON: I don't want to pressure him at such an infant stage of his development, but I hope he'll carry on my legacy.

For a second the snow machine works. ALL react with joy.

DAVE: Well, look at that.

JASON: Now that is what I'm talking about. Let's see if we can replicate it.

JASON and DAVE go back to work.

MARGOT: (*to LISA*) So are you a teacher yet, then?

LISA: What?

MARGOT: That's still what you're planning on doing, right? Teaching? I remember you mentioning –

LISA: Oh. Well, yeah. I think so. I mean I still have five years left of my Ph.D. so –

MARGOT: Five years!

LISA: Oh yeah. It's a seven-year program, I'm two years in, so I kinda feel like my job might just be going to school forever, you know?

MARGOT: Five more years.

DAVE: You like it, though, science, physics, right?

LISA: My thesis explores the structure of clusters of galaxies.

JASON: So you get to look into a telescope a lot?

LISA: Sometimes. Mostly I type stuff into this computer software and watch stars move around my computer screen. Oh, and I read a lot.

MARGOT: But you like it?

LISA: Love it.

MARGOT: Gets you out of this town.[1]

LISA: It does ...

---

1   *"This town" can be replaced with the name of the town the play is being produced in.*

MARGOT: I know how that was always a priority of yours: getting out of here.

LISA: It was, but –

MARGOT: Abandoning all relationships, to the point of being unsure if old friends are giving birth to new life.

The snow machine is successful again.

JASON: Perfect. Now we have enough time for phase two, where we go downstairs and act as though we were there all the while.

DAVE: You mean enjoy the wedding reception? I think I can do that.

JASON: Exactly. Act like that. And Lisa?

LISA: Yeah?

JASON: Are you staying up here?

LISA: I don't know, I mean, I wasn't planning to, but –

JASON: If you do, don't touch anything.

LISA: Okay.

DAVE: For your own safety, maybe. There may be more hot surfaces in there.

JASON: And for aesthetic reasons.

LISA: Got it.

JASON: I will see you up here in three quarters of an hour!

JASON and DAVE exit.

MARGOT: You know what, I think I should go back down, too.

LISA: Margot, I feel like I should –

MARGOT: Lisa, it's okay.

LISA: But I wanted to tell you that –

MARGOT: It's fine, Lisa. It's good you're here at Carl's wedding.

LISA: Is it? Margot, I –

MARGOT: Even if you're avoiding everybody.

LISA: Oh, I'm not avoiding –

MARGOT: Upstairs in the hallway on your own.

LISA: Yeah.

MARGOT: Here. Keep this drink. Lisa, my dear, I have a feeling you might be up here for a little while.

> *MARGOT exits.*

SCENE 4
GALAXIES ABOVE US

LISA starts to cry uncontrollably again.

LISA: Uh! No crying allowed.

> *MICHELLE and HEATHER enter, making out. Not wanting to be seen, LISA hides in the washroom. Still making out, MICHELLE and HEATHER try classroom doors to see if they can get inside.*

MICHELLE: Oh my god, we're making out again.

HEATHER: Yup.

MICHELLE: How does this keep happening?

HEATHER: I don't know.

> *MICHELLE and HEATHER continue to make out while HEATHER tries more doors.*

MICHELLE: I just wanted to say I think it's very cool that you're wearing a backpack to a wedding.

HEATHER: Thank you.

MICHELLE: I haven't ever really thought of backpacks as part of wedding attire, but you, you saw that it could be.

HEATHER: Well, this wedding needed a little backpack, I think.

MICHELLE: You're completely right.

> *HEATHER wraps her foot around MICHELLE and they almost fall over laughing. HEATHER's shoe falls off.*

MICHELLE: Oh my god. Do you remember that time in the Murphy's basement when J did something mean to me, and you were comforting me with your shoe?

HEATHER: Was it that time when he ripped the head off your teddy bear to make it into one of his art projects?

MICHELLE: No.

HEATHER: Was it when he didn't go to your ballet recital out of protest against eating disorders?

MICHELLE: Nope.

HEATHER: When he drew a huge peace sign in permanent marker on your living-room wall and Grandma Margot almost murdered you?

MICHELLE: No! It was when he convinced me to burn off a section of my hair so that we could both have the same awful almost-bald spot on our heads for prom.

HEATHER: You looked so bad.

MICHELLE: Yeah? Well, you didn't seem to mind.

HEATHER: I was good at hiding my disgust.

MICHELLE: Well, I remember you making me feel better in the Murphy's basement. Pretending your shoe was a ... dog?

HEATHER: Oh no! I remember, the shoe was a walrus.

HEATHER barks like a walrus.

MICHELLE: You were so good at that. Making me feel better.

HEATHER: I was, wasn't I?

HEATHER and MICHELLE make out again. LISA comes out of the washroom and attempts to sneak downstairs.

MICHELLE: Lisa!

LISA: Don't let me stop you!

MICHELLE: Hey, it's Lisa.

HEATHER: Lisa? Hey, Lisa girl.

LISA: Hi you two.

MICHELLE: Haven't seen much of you today.

LISA: Have you seen much of anything besides ...

MICHELLE: Oh. Uh ...

HEATHER: Yeah.

LISA: So this still happens? I had no idea.

HEATHER: Yup.

MICHELLE: No.

LISA: It's okay. I don't care. I'm just surprised.

HEATHER: We haven't seen you in a while. You've been avoiding us.

LISA: I have not.

HEATHER: You have.

LISA: No, really, I –

MICHELLE: We know, the famous writer's been keeping you busy.

LISA: Yes.

MICHELLE: And school.

LISA: Yes, that too.

   HEATHER looks at the unwrapped present.

HEATHER: And a box with a skull in it?

LISA: Present. Wedding present for Carl. And Gabrielle.

HEATHER: You know, usually people wrap those up, right?

LISA: I've heard that, yeah.

HEATHER: I always thought you were more into the galaxies
  above us than the dead things left behind us.

LISA: I am. But right now they don't seem all that
  different, somehow.

MICHELLE: You remember that time when we tried to build a
  spaceship on my grandma's lawn?

LISA: I do.

HEATHER: I think we would have made good aliens.

MICHELLE: My grandma's grass still won't grow in that spot
  where we lit the kerosene lamp.

HEATHER: Kaboom!

LISA: Oh no. Is Margot still mad about that? She seems to really
  care a lot about her lawn.

MICHELLE: I get to hear about it every spring. And now that I have a little guy of my own, Grandma keeps threatening that she'll do the same to our own lawn when Leo gets big enough.

LISA: Leo! I haven't met baby Leo yet. You must be out of your mind in love with that little guy.

MICHELLE: Leo's so cute. I mean, I may be a little biased because I think I'm cute and he looks exactly like me, but really he's for sure the most adorable child in the world.

HEATHER: He really is cute.

LISA: Look guys, I hate to ask, but just in case I run into him, does J know?

HEATHER: J who?

MICHELLE: I don't think he doesn't know.

LISA: I don't know what that means.

HEATHER: He has no idea that this happens or has ever happened.

MICHELLE: Hey. I mean, he's not stupid.

HEATHER: I didn't say he was.

MICHELLE: But we don't need to talk about it, because he wouldn't care.

LISA: He wouldn't?

MICHELLE: No.

LISA: At all?

HEATHER: Lisa –

MICHELLE: He wouldn't because it's, you know …

LISA: What?

MICHELLE: Well, he wouldn't see it as cheating.

LISA: He wouldn't?

HEATHER: Lisa, it's okay –

LISA: Why wouldn't he see this as cheating?

MICHELLE: He'd probably be into it. I mean, you know how it is.

LISA: Wow.

MICHELLE: What?

LISA: Nothing.

MICHELLE: You know what I mean. Lisa, you definitely know
what I mean.

LISA: Uh, well, sorry, Michelle, but not really.

MICHELLE: Oh. Okay.

LISA: But I haven't been around. I'm missing so much I probably
don't have the whole picture on this one.

MICHELLE: Well, obviously not, then. I guess you better not let
Carl keep you away again, okay? So you don't miss so much.

LISA: Oh, that's not why I …

MICHELLE: You what? Haven't been around since he and Gabs
got together?

HEATHER: Lisa, she doesn't –

LISA: It's fine.

MICHELLE: Well, I think I'm going to go down to Leo.

LISA: I hear he's untethered down there, so –

MICHELLE: Right.

HEATHER: Michelle –

MICHELLE: Back to my family.

MICHELLE exits.

SCENE 5
LACTOSE INTOLERANT

LISA and HEATHER watch MICHELLE leave.

LISA: Oh my god. Was she always like that? I don't remember her always being like that.

HEATHER: Pretty much, yeah.

LISA: How does she do that? I mean the way her mind works.

HEATHER: Yeah. It's interesting.

LISA: I'm so sorry. I mean, what she said was –

HEATHER: I know.

LISA: Are you okay?

HEATHER: I'm so good. Gotta love love.

LISA: Love is really dumb. What's the point of a wedding again?

HEATHER reaches into her backpack and pulls out a book.

HEATHER: Okay. I'm about to show you something super embarrassing.

LISA: Okay.

HEATHER: You ready for this?

LISA: Yeah.

HEATHER: At J and Michelle's wedding, I stole this. Do you remember this?

LISA: Vaguely.

HEATHER: It's a book, a registry, a list of names of all guests who came to the wedding. Like a B & B guest book where you write your name and where you're from, like Paris or Sudbury or Berlin. And a note beside, like, "Great spot! Beautiful views!" Or, "Loved the blueberry pancakes!"

LISA: Right.

HEATHER: So Margot had all their guests write their names as they came in.

LISA: Susanne and Phillip Fines. This is Michelle and Carl's cousin, right?

HEATHER: Right.

LISA: Susanne and Phillip Fines. From Lucknow, Ontario. "You couldn't have picked a prettier day. What a fun band! They played the best mix of all the classics and were a party starter for sure! Everything was perfect. Congratulations!" Jeffy and Jolene Van Houten. From Ottawa, Ontario.

HEATHER: That's J's sister.

LISA: Oh right. The one who spent the end of the night swimming in the pond.

HEATHER: Yeah, her.

LISA: "Well, you did it! You're married! Wooooooooooooooooooo oooooooooooooooooo! Everybody loved the eats and thanks for not being stingy on the bar. Will recommend to our friends."

Will recommend what to her friends?

HEATHER: I have no idea.

LISA: Faith Lafleur and Bran Morris. From Toronto, Ontario. These are J's friends from college, right?

HEATHER: I think so, yeah.

LISA: "It was beautiful. You guys thought of everything. Congratulations, and we'll see you this summer at the cottage. Lots of love."

HEATHER: This has been living in the blocked-up old laundry chute in my bathroom for the past five years. At J and Michelle's wedding, I meant to just go and read these on my own in a quiet corner, you know. I was feeling anti-social and getting super drunk, so I thought that was a safe course of action, but instead I ended up reading this for half an hour on my own and, well –

LISA: Bad decision.

HEATHER: Yeah, and I may have written over a few entries.

LISA: What did you write?

LISA: "Yeah right. Fuck their love. I love for real. Stand down, imposters." Oh, Heather. "Lift the veil, motherfuckers. There's only pain? Big fucking pain." Really? Heather. Jesus.

HEATHER: Yeah. I was a mess. I was also so embarrassed that I actually did that, I ended up stealing this book so nobody could ever see it. I thought about just ripping out these pages, but I think that would have been almost worse, because then a bunch of people would seem like they didn't even sign the thing. So I decided it was better it went completely missing. And so I ended up going home without telling anybody why.

LISA: I remember, like, a week later you telling me you got too drunk and wandered home. You said you didn't even remember it, that you woke up in bed and didn't know how you got there.

HEATHER: I *said* I didn't even remember it. I remember every second.

LISA: I just thought you were a little drunk and upset, but I had no idea.

HEATHER: As soon as I got home, I put it in the old laundry chute in my bathroom. The next day I bought a picture of a whale in a bathtub from Walmart to cover up the door.

LISA: Okay.

HEATHER: But every time I go, you know, it's right in front of me, winking at me. I know this sounds crazy, but I swear to god, the whale winks, Lisa. I thought about getting a new picture, to swap it out, but the whale, it knows too much now. It's better it stays with me.

LISA: So why bring this here, then?

HEATHER: I don't know. I thought maybe this being our old high school, I could hide it somewhere here instead, because it's killing me at home. And it's another Burk wedding, so it felt appropriate, somehow.

LISA: Okay. We can do that. I think that sounds like a good mission.

HEATHER: I've been looking, though, Leese, and now that this place has been renovated it's so clean. Do you remember how this place used to feel like there were corners to hide in everywhere?

LISA: Yup.

HEATHER: Modernism destroyed hide-and-seek.

LISA: Yeah. It's so pretty and clean now. I kind of hate it.

HEATHER: Me too. So I say we should build another spaceship and blast off into the outer reaches of our galaxy and hide it there. No Michelle and Js there, I hear.

LISA: I'm down.

HEATHER: And no Carls either, I don't think. Or famous writers?

LISA: Do you have Dave's number?

HEATHER: I sure do.

LISA: I think we could use Dave's help right about now. You in the mood?

HEATHER texts DAVE.

HEATHER: And he's on his way up.

LISA: That is good news.

HEATHER puts the book back in her backpack.

LISA: Have you ever thought about telling her?

HEATHER: Telling Michelle what, exactly?

LISA: That you love her. Maybe things would change if she knew.

HEATHER: Change to what? No Michelle. At least I have, or somewhat have her, now.

LISA: I guess. But maybe she would …

HEATHER: What? Abandon her family and pick me?

LISA: You never know.

HEATHER: I mean, I daydream about it.

LISA: About telling her that you love her?

HEATHER: Yeah.

LISA: And?

HEATHER: And what our wedding day would look like.

LISA: Oh yikes.

HEATHER: Oh yeah.

LISA: So? Tell me about it.

HEATHER: Well, J would officiate. He'd be so okay with our total love that he would get a licence to bring us together till death do us part.

LISA: Wow.

HEATHER: And we'd come in together. Like, we'd both walk each other in. And then we'd fly up to the altar.

LISA: Fly, like –

HEATHER: Really fly. We'd have Peter Pan machines. You're not going to believe this, but I've taken up circus. Just in case.

LISA: What do you mean? Like, going to the circus?

HEATHER: No. Like being in one. Or practising as if I was going to be in one, one day. But really, practising for a circus-themed wedding, if I'm being honest.

LISA: This is elaborate.

HEATHER: See. I can now do this.

HEATHER does an acrobatic move. DAVE enters.

DAVE: And what am I walking into here?

HEATHER: Dave. Oh my god. I don't know if I've ever been so happy to see you.

DAVE: I'm liking you two right now as well.

LISA: I only have ten bucks on me. I hope that's okay.

DAVE: Plenty. (*offering a vape*) I got this guy if you want to stay in here?

LISA: Nobody will care?

DAVE: It's still a real grey issue these days, but I don't see anybody around, so ...

HEATHER: I say why not.

DAVE: Yeah, screw it!

LISA: Okay. Screw it!

GABRIELLE enters.

DAVE: Hello, pretty bride.

GABRIELLE: Hey, guys. I, uh – well I saw Dave come up, here so I thought maybe you were –

LISA: Oh. Sorry, Gabrielle. We can totally stop.
We didn't mean to –

GABRIELLE: No, no, no. I was actually wondering if I could join you?

DAVE: Oh yeah!

HEATHER: Of course.

LISA: Oh. Okay.

GABRIELLE: Thanks. It's kinda cool doing this in our old school, eh?

HEATHER: Very cool.

LISA: I love that you guys decided to get married here.

HEATHER: It's very romantic.

GABRIELLE: I didn't really know you guys then.

LISA: No.

HEATHER: That was probably just because you're a few years younger. You know how that is. Hanging out with a fourteen-year-old when you're seventeen seems impossible, somehow.

GABRIELLE: I used to think you two were really cool, you know.

LISA: Us?

GABRIELLE: I was completely intimidated by you.

DAVE: Well then, you all must be very intimidated by me.

GABRIELLE: Terrified.

HEATHER: Oh! Watch out! Here comes old Dave!

LISA: You are very scary.

GABRIELLE: Dave, you must be so happy about legalization?

DAVE: You know, pretty bride, you're right. I've been fighting for my right to hold this sucker and make sure you can hold this sucker and make sure you can hold this sucker and you can hold this sucker for a really long time, you know? I should be very excited that now we all just can.

LISA: But you're not?

DAVE: Do you remember Jordy Pillon? Well, actually he went to this place with me a million years ago, so how could you little kiddos? Well, poor Jordan Pillon, just after he turned eighteen, bought this girl he liked, Maggie Wright, a dime bag and Maggie Wright stupidly left it in her locker. I think it was actually on this floor somewhere, over there, maybe, and Maggie Wright's locker was searched and then in the office her memory was searched for where this little baggie from her locker came from.

HEATHER: Did she tell them?

DAVE: Yup. And that was the day poor Jordy Pillon's life completely changed, my friends. He was charged with trafficking, if you can believe it. On his permanent record.

GABRIELLE: Shit.

DAVE: Shit is right, because until that point little Jordy had a clean slate, did well in school, even wanted to be a schoolteacher, but all that went bye-bye. You can't be a schoolteacher with pot on your record.

HEATHER: Well now, with the new rules, there may be less of that, right?

DAVE: Yup, and that's good tick.

LISA: But what about Jordy Pillon?

DAVE: Exactly. My heart just can't stop thinking, "What about poor Jordy Pillon?" There's nothing anybody can do about him.

GABRIELLE: (*pointing to the art project*) Hey guys, what is all this stuff?

DAVE: This, pretty bride, this is something you have to pretend you have not seen.

GABRIELLE: Oh yeah? Why?

DAVE: It's invisible.

GABRIELLE: Is it?

DAVE: You will be surprised to see this again in a few minutes.

GABRIELLE: Oh fun! That I can do. I should go back downstairs then, shouldn't I?

HEATHER: You are the bride.

DAVE: The beautiful bride.

GABRIELLE: Thanks for the time-out.

GABRIELLE exits. LISA starts crying.

DAVE: Whoa. Lisa, you okay?

HEATHER: Are you crying?

LISA: Oh no. I'm sorry, guys.

DAVE: Jordy would appreciate the sentiment. I get it. It's a sad predicament.

HEATHER: I don't think this is about Jordy, Dave. Is it about Carl?

LISA: No.

HEATHER: I guess it must be Jordy, then. Did you know him?

LISA: No. No. I – uh. I'm sorry. This just keeps happening lately. I can't seem to control my eyes anymore.

HEATHER: What's going on?

LISA: I, uh –

DAVE: Yeah?

LISA: Well, it's –

HEATHER: What is it, Leese?

LISA: I'm lactose intolerant.

DAVE: Oh shit.

HEATHER: I'm not sure I'm following.

LISA: I know. It's weird, but last week I found out I'm lactose intolerant and I started to cry. "Weep" would be a better description, I guess, or "rain," maybe, because I couldn't seem to make myself stop.

DAVE: Let it rain.

LISA: Or stop involuntarily, either.

HEATHER: That's screwed up, Lisa.

LISA: I know! I had to cancel my first meeting with my thesis advisor, a woman who single-handedly inspired my pursuit of science, of learning more about those blinky twinkles up there in the sky.

DAVE: No.

LISA: Her work in galaxy systems was what awoke something in me. Pushed my dream to the surface and, you know, she's a woman, so that helped, too. Seeing someone other than white-haired man number one or tall, skinny, box-glasses professor-man number two with a lectern in front of her was real for me.

HEATHER: I get that, but –

LISA: And I was supposed to have my first one-to-one meeting with her and I couldn't, because my eyes wouldn't stop crying.

DAVE: Your body, the betrayer.

LISA: Lactose intolerant! Why couldn't I be allergic to something else? Anything else. Bees. I wouldn't mind avoiding them for the rest of my life. Or peanuts. That would be fine. Me and every kid born after the year 2000 would have something in common to talk about. Or shellfish, avocados, salt even, for god's sake, but not lactose. Not milk.

DAVE: I really like milk, too.

HEATHER: Lisa, I mean I'm trying here, but –

LISA: The word "galaxy," like many words, derives from Greek. The Greek word "galaxias," where it all begins, means simply this: milky. I'm allergic to galaxies. My thesis is on galaxies.

HEATHER and DAVE: Oh.

LISA: Eventually my eyes stopped raining, like rain does, and I called, but my thesis advisor had already left for Switzerland for the summer. I got home and Max –

HEATHER: The famous writer?

LISA: Yeah, he told me I was being "irrational and weak-spirited." I don't exactly know what came over me, but I just went into the backyard and started a bonfire. Not a big one at first, but then I started going into the house and grabbing everything and burning it. Everything. Max was going nuts and yelled that I was losing my mind and maybe I was. He drove off into the night. I just sat by the campfire until morning. And then I had to put on this dress and get on a plane, and came here to Carl's wedding.

DAVE: You do kind of smell like campfire.

HEATHER: Lisa, I'm so sorry. Are you still, I mean, does Carl still mean that much to you?

LISA: He didn't. For a very, very long time, he didn't.

HEATHER: But he does again?

LISA: I don't know. I've been feeling so nostalgic lately. Do you guys ever feel like you've made all the wrong decisions in life and there's an alternate life for you that you should be living instead, but it's too late?

HEATHER: Every day.

DAVE: Today wouldn't have happened if yesterday didn't either and I like today.

HEATHER: Lisa, you are the girl who everyone thinks of as having made it. You're out there being successful and accomplished.

LISA: Really?

HEATHER: Oh yeah.

LISA: I don't feel that way at all. In fact, I feel like a fool.

HEATHER: A fool?

LISA: I know. It's maybe an outdated word, but I think it fits me perfectly right now. A fool.

> *DAVE starts to sing his version of "Everybody Plays the Fool" or a similar song about being foolish. It kind of comes out of nowhere at first, but then HEATHER and LISA start to get into it too, letting it connect to their own lives, giving them a little joy in their misery. They sing along and dance. HEATHER ends the song with a little flourish.*

SCENE 6
WHITE WEDDING

JASON enters during the last little bit of song from the previous scene.

JASON: I think you guys are ready to go on tour.

HEATHER: Oh my god, J!

LISA: J, you scared the crap out of me!

DAVE: He is really stealthy.

JASON: I'm in anguish.

LISA: As usual.

JASON: There are not enough power outlets up here for my purposes. But Dave and Lisa, can I get you to stand by for our mission?

DAVE: Aye-aye, Captain.

LISA: Standing by.

JASON: And Heather.

HEATHER: Yeah?

JASON: I didn't know you could sing like that.

HEATHER: Um. Thank you.

JASON: I might have to incorporate those skills into this project as well.

HEATHER: Okay.

JASON: Are you able to learn quickly or perhaps on the fly?

HEATHER: Maybe. I think so.

JASON: I have faith in you.

HEATHER: Thank you.

JASON: Have you seen my wife around?

HEATHER: Uh ...

LISA: She went down a while ago to Leo.

JASON: Right. Good. Our child, but she should be arriving back up here shortly.

HEATHER: Michelle's coming back up here right now?

JASON: If she finds a person willing to hold our baby.

MARGOT and MICHELLE enter.

MARGOT: Hey, J. I found an extension cord for you to use. The caterer said they'll need it back by tomorrow morning.

JASON: Excellent. I am no longer in anguish.

MARGOT: I think we got a minute or two. Carl said he'd send the photographer up ahead to warn us.

MICHELLE: Leo's out and the Murphys said they'd watch him for a little bit, so I'm free if you need me, babe.

JASON: Yes. Perfect. I'll get you to hold this.

JASON hands MICHELLE a light to hold.

LISA: Wait!

LISA is very concerned because she's worried the light will be hot, so she grabs it first, but it isn't hot at all. ALL except JASON and DAVE are confused.

LISA: It seems safe.

MICHELLE: Thank you?

JASON: And Margot, can you grab this?

JASON hands MARGOT a light to hold.

MARGOT: I don't know, what does Lisa think?

LISA: I think it should be okay.

JASON: And Lisa, I'll get you to hold this.

JASON hands LISA a light to hold.

LISA: Sure.

After two false alarms, LISA grabs the object not worrying if it's hot, and it is surprisingly warm.

JASON: Dave, you know what you gotta do, and Heather, I'll get you to sing along with him, yeah?

HEATHER: Yeah.

ANNIE enters.

ANNIE: It's time!

JASON: Okay, everyone. On my count. One, two ...

CARL and GABRIELLE enter.

JASON: Three!

ALL join DAVE to sing a reprise of the third wedding song from scene 1 while the snow machine produces snow, which flies around beautifully.

GABRIELLE: Oh my god.

CARL: Do you like it?

GABRIELLE: You did this for me.

CARL: I did this for you. I'm sorry we couldn't have a winter wedding, so I hope this is an okay substitute?

GABRIELLE: You are so sneaky. I am floored. I love it.

CARL: You're smiling.

GABRIELLE: Of course I'm smiling!

ANNIE: So get in there. We need some photos of you in the snow!

GABRIELLE: Deal!

CARL and GABRIELLE start dancing in the snow. ANNIE takes photos.

ANNIE: Good, good. But we need to get that backpack off our lovely singer there.

HEATHER: Oh, uh. Actually.

ANNIE: I'll just put it over there.

ANNIE puts the backpack to the side.

ANNIE: Perfect ... Now join them!

HEATHER goes in to dance in the snow.

ANNIE: I love it. Now let's switch the song to something twirly.

DAVE plays something "twirly" on the guitar.

ANNIE: Good. And can we just get the bride to twirl in the snow?

ALL move to the side so GABRIELLE can twirl in the snow.

ANNIE: Lovely.

MICHELLE, joking around, goes to HEATHER's backpack and opens it. She finds the book. JASON sees it. HEATHER sees it.

HEATHER: No!

HEATHER grabs the book out of MICHELLE's hands. The music stops and ALL stare at HEATHER.

JASON: Heather, is that our wedding reception registry book?

HEATHER: Yes.

JASON: Margot almost murdered a caterer because she thought he packed it up with the plates when he left our wedding.

HEATHER: I know.

JASON: I specifically asked everyone if they knew anything about the disappearance of that book.

HEATHER: Yes, you did.

MARGOT: So why do you have it, Heather?

HEATHER: I don't know.

JASON: You don't know why you have that book?

HEATHER: I –

MICHELLE: She's deranged, J. She obviously is really lonely, and it was too much for her that night. So she had to steal a little bit of our happiness to make herself feel better. Right, Heather?

DAVE: Oh, cold.

JASON: Is that what happened, Heather?

HEATHER: I – yes. That is what happened.

LISA: No.

JASON: No?

LISA: No.

MICHELLE: Lisa!

MARGOT: Michelle, what is going on here?

LISA: J, I think it's time that you know something –

HEATHER: Lisa stop, it's okay –

LISA: No, it's not okay.

JASON: What, Lisa? What do I need to know?

LISA: Heather and Michelle …

MARGOT: Oh my god.

MICHELLE: Lisa, don't.

JASON: Don't what?

DAVE: Holy shit.

LISA: They are –

HEATHER: We're in love, J.

JASON: What?

MICHELLE: No, we're not. No we're not.

HEATHER: Yes, we are. Michelle, I love you and you love me. It's not perfect, but –

MICHELLE: No, I don't. I don't love you. She's crazy, J, she's …

JASON: Michelle.

MICHELLE: She doesn't know what she's talking about.

JASON: Michelle, do you love Heather?

MICHELLE: I, uh …

JASON: Oh, this is not good.

MICHELLE: It's uh, very confusing …

JASON: And this has been happening since?

HEATHER: Since high school.

JASON: And you all must have known.

MARGOT: I certainly did not know this.

DAVE: No idea, my friend.

CARL: I thought it was over, bud.

LISA: J, I'm sorry, I just thought you should –

JASON: I now know. We all now know.

MICHELLE: But I'm not the only one here with a secret, J. Lisa is just as bad.

LISA: What?

MICHELLE: She is also in love.

LISA: No, I'm not.

MARGOT: Michelle, let's think about our actions here.

MICHELLE: I don't care.

DAVE: Whoa, this is going to a bad place. I feel some rot festering here.

MICHELLE: Lisa is in love with –

LISA: Michelle, please!

MICHELLE: Carl. Lisa is in love with Carl.

GABRIELLE: What?

MICHELLE: And Carl is in love with Lisa.

CARL: Oh, mother.

GABRIELLE: What is she talking about, Carl?

CARL: Gabs, she's joking. Right, Michelle? You're joking.

MICHELLE: I am not joking.

CARL: This is my wedding, Michelle. Just because your marriage is a sham doesn't mean mine is.

GABRIELLE: I can't believe this is happening.

MARGOT: Gabrielle, Michelle's obviously very upset and just saying the first thing that comes to her mind.

CARL: Lisa is not in love with me. Right, Leese? Not in love.

LISA: I am not in love with you.

CARL: See? And I am not in love with her.

LISA: I don't love you.

CARL: And I don't love you either.

GABRIELLE: Okay!

CARL: Gabs, I –

GABRIELLE: No, I get it, not in love!

CARL: Exactly.

GABRIELLE: Uh. Okay. I still think I might need a minute alone. I get it. No love, but my wedding day, you know. I thought something bad would happen, but I was hoping I would be wrong.

CARL: Gabs, but the snow. I made it snow for you. I love you.

GABRIELLE: I know, and it's beautiful. Thank you, I just – give me a minute.

CARL: Gabs, wait, you should not –

GABRIELLE goes downstairs.

CARL: (*to MICHELLE*) You, you ruined my wedding. Michelle, you are such a brat. I can't believe you.

MICHELLE: Carl, I was just –

MARGOT: Michelle, you have some issues to deal with right now.

MICHELLE: Issues?

MARGOT: I think I should leave you alone with your issues. Carl, come on, let's go after that bride that's too good for you. And you, little girl, will fix this.

MICHELLE: Grandma, I ...

MARGOT: Fix this now.

CARL and MARGOT exit.

JASON: I feel like such a fool.

DAVE: There's a lot of that going around, brother.

JASON: Michelle, why didn't you just tell me?

MICHELLE: I don't know.

JASON: We have a child downstairs.

MICHELLE: I know.

HEATHER: You can punch me if you want.

JASON: Heather.

HEATHER: In the face. I won't move.

JASON: I'm going to tell you to fuck off. Fuck off, Heather.

HEATHER: Okay.

JASON: I'm just – I'm gonna take Leo home.

MICHELLE: Can I come with you?

JASON: I would rather not. Dave, I think we need to drink now.

DAVE: I can do that.

MICHELLE: But, J –

JASON: I realize you are not a good woman, Michelle. Not a good woman at all.

DAVE and JASON exit.

MICHELLE: You ruined my life!

HEATHER: I'm sorry, I just –

MICHELLE: No, not you. Lisa.

LISA: Me?

MICHELLE: You were feeling miserable coming here with your stupid more-important-Lisa-problems and just had to dump all that shit and bile and puke all over us.

LISA: But I –

MICHELLE: Oh my god. My life is ruined.

LISA: If your life is ruined, that is your fault, Michelle. And by the way, I think you just destroyed my relationship with my best friend. Thanks for that.

MICHELLE: The all-important Lisa problems. Heather, can we just go?

LISA: Yeah right, like she wants to go with you right now.

MICHELLE: Heather?

HEATHER: Sorry, Leese.

LISA: Oh. Wow.

HEATHER: I know.

LISA: This is so messed up.

HEATHER: Yeah, I know, but it's mine. You got yours, and I got mine.

LISA: Okay.

HEATHER: Are you going to be okay up here on your own?

LISA: Peachy.

HEATHER: Welcome home.

    HEATHER and MICHELLE exit.

SCENE 7
NOT CRYING

LISA is on her own and not crying.

LISA: Oh my god. I'm not crying. I'm not crying.

CARL enters.

LISA: I'm not crying, Carl.

CARL: That's good. I think. I came up here to make sure you're okay.

LISA: I'm okay. I can't believe it. I'm okay.

CARL: Good.

LISA: Oh, Carl. It's your wedding.

CARL: Yeah.

LISA: It's your wedding, and I ruined it.

CARL: No, you didn't ruin it, Leese. Pretty close, but –

LISA: I did, though. I came here and it got screwed up. I screwed it up. I'm a screw-up.

CARL: You know you're basically the opposite of a screw-up, right?

LISA: You really think that?

CARL: Everyone thinks of you as having your shit together.

LISA: That is very funny to me.

CARL: Maybe that will change after tonight, though, I don't know.

LISA: I don't, you know. You know that I don't …

CARL: Don't what?

LISA: Don't …

CARL: Love me?

LISA: I don't.

CARL: Good.

LISA: Oh, I mean I love you. You're Carl, and I will always love you, but –

CARL: And I will always love you, but –

LISA: I love galaxies.

CARL: Yes, you do.

LISA: But I just found out I'm lactose intolerant, and I just had to spread that misery to others, I guess. Maybe Michelle is right.

CARL starts laughing.

LISA: Carl?

CARL is really laughing.

LISA: Carl? Why are you laughing?

CARL: That's funny.

LISA: You think that's funny? My misery is funny to you?

CARL: It's really, really funny, Leese.

LISA: It is really, really funny.

CARL: Lactose intolerant.

LISA: I know!

CARL: You! Now that's funny! Because if you're lactose intolerant, you're intolerant of galaxies!

LISA: Yes! See. You got it right away. This is why I love you, Carl. But not that kind of "I love you," Carl. I swear I don't love you like that, Jesus.

CARL: I know. It's okay.

LISA: I'm really happy you got married.

CARL: Me too.

LISA: Gabrielle is actually super cool.

CARL: She's like my dream girl.

LISA: I'm impressed you got someone so cool.

CARL: Me too.

LISA: I mean, I didn't think that was going to happen for you.

CARL: Thanks. I hear the writer is kinda odd or cold or –

LISA: Some may say that.

CARL: But not you?

LISA: I think he's really brilliant.

CARL: Of course you do.

LISA: You know, I think I'm still going to try to drink milk, even if it hurts.

CARL: That sounds about right. I gotta get back to my wife, Leese.

LISA: Okay.

CARL: But are you going to be in town for a while?

LISA: Maybe. Yeah. Maybe a little while.

CARL: Good. I'll call you when I get back from my honeymoon.

LISA: Deal.

CARL exits.

LISA: Oh Carl, you forgot your skull!

Blackout.

The End

Post
Alice

Left to right: Aubree Erickson, Heather Marie Annis, Ellen Denny, and Siobhan O'Malley in Here For Now Theatre's production of *Post Alice*, July–August 2021

Photograph by Claire Scott

PRODUCTION HISTORY

Post Alice was first produced from July 27 to August 15, 2021, by Here For Now Theatre at the Bruce Hotel in Stratford, Ontario, with the following cast and crew:

WENLOCK: Ellen Denny
BELLE: Siobhan O'Malley
ONORA: Heather Marie Annis
EDIE: Aubree Erickson

Director: Fiona Mongillo
Cultural Consultant: Terre Chartrand
Musical Arranger: Mark Payne
Costume Designer: Monique Lund
Technical Director: Wendy Ewert

CHARACTERS

WENLOCK: Twenty-nine to thirty-four (*a little younger than the others*). Lives in Vienna, but is from Huron County. A writer and filmmaker. Wrote and directed a short film that was presented at a number of artsy European film festivals. She's in the middle of working on another film about Mistie Murray. She doesn't visit home much. Spends a lot of time in her head analyzing her past. Belle is her sister. In love with Onora. Name inspired by Alice Munro's short story "Wenlock Edge."

BELLE: Thirty to thirty-five (*same age as Onora and Edie*). Understated, depressed, funny. Everything she says is a half-joke. Lives on a large, rundown farm which was her father's. Loves to read and works at the library. Has many unpursued ambitions. Recently, she found out she has cancer (*osteosarcoma*) and needs to have surgery to remove her leg. Her husband, a motocross rider she started dating in high school, recently left her. As a child, she was obsessed with the Mistie Murray story. Wenlock is her sister. Name inspired by Alice Munro's short story "Train."

ONORA: Thirty to thirty-five (*same age as Belle and Edie*). A deeply compassionate person, at times to a fault. She comes from a wealthy family that owns property in Goderich, Ontario, which she manages. Her father is Haudenosaunee, but rarely talks about family on his side, whom Onora has never met due to a tragedy which fractured his family long ago. She is currently grappling with her own identity, but she can only scratch the surface of her feelings with her settler childhood friends. As a child, she was obsessed with the Mistie Murray story. She is still cautiously in love with Wenlock. Name inspired by Alice Munro's short story "Pride."

EDIE: Thirty to thirty-five (*same age as Onora and Belle*). Feels like the oldest of the group. Loud, fun, a bit of a shit disturber and can go too far with her sarcasm at times. She hides her fear and trauma with humour. As a child, she was obsessed with the Mistie Murray story. A search-and-rescue pilot married to another pilot. Name inspired by Alice Munro's short story "How I Met My Husband."

SETTING

The setting is Belle's rundown backyard on a small, dilapidated farm somewhere in Huron County. This is the same farm she and Wenlock grew up on together with their now-deceased parents. Belle's partner Jackson Maynard also lived here for nearly two decades, until recently. There's a lot of history here. The audience sees a firepit and some tired lawn chairs.

At times, the play takes place in a different place or time than that of the main narrative, but these moments are intended to be depicted abstractly. The set should stay the same throughout. Design elements for lighting, sound, and projection could help support the passage of time throughout the evening and indicate switches in place and time. Audience imagination is likely best to fill in the blanks for the other settings, but miming of props is strongly discouraged. The following key realistic props should be used to ground the characters in the world of the play:
- the envelope
- the whittled leg
- the first-aid kit
- the knife
- the axe
- the small tree Edie carries in
- beers
- sandwiches
- the box of puppet supplies and books from the library.

TIME

The play takes place over the span of one evening with flashbacks to other places and times.

Please note that this play makes reference to sexual assault and Missing and Murdered Indigenous Women and Girls.

SCENE 1
SUNSET

*A backyard with a firepit in Huron County. BELLE enters
with a beer. She sits in a lawn chair and stares into the
empty firepit. A dirt bike revs in the distance. BELLE looks
for the sound but can't find it. She picks up a piece of wood
placed beside her chair. It has been whittled to look like a
leg. BELLE continues to whittle the leg and sings.*

BELLE:
(*singing*) Fire's burning
Fire's burning
Draw nearer
Draw nearer
In the glowing
In the glowing
We're all fucked in the end.

Fire's burning
Fire's burning
Draw nearer
Draw nearer
In the glowing
In the glowing
We all die alone.

*WENLOCK, ONORA, and EDIE run in through the audience,
laughing, in another time and space. They run to the edge
of the stage or playing space as if running up to the edge of
the Goderich bluffs.*

WENLOCK: We were out of breath standing at the edge of the
bluffs, looking out onto Lake Huron. We were all somewhere
around fifteen, sixteen, and we had never done this before, this
thing that tourists do when they come to our town. You watch
one sunset at the bottom, on the stupidly beautiful beach, and
then you race up to here, where the trees part just in time to

watch another one, hues fading into that royal-burnt-purple in the sky, in the lake. God, I hated it.

We were laughing with every bit of ourselves, because it's hilarious to do something that you think is annoying that other people find so meaningful. It's like an inside joke where you can secretly love both the irony and the genuine beauty of a moment in life all at once. But don't you dare tip too far into sentimentality, because things that other people like can't make you original, powerful, yourself. And that's all we wanted to be.

There was something in me that knew I wouldn't be there much longer. That the town was letting me go. I could already feel it turning its back on me. And that turning, that twisting, reminded me of her just then, of Mistie Murray, never found. I wondered if she ever felt this way, twisted and sentimental, brave and breathless, facing a Huron County sunset.

I remember looking over at Onora, in love with how perfect she looked in that pink tiger-striped bathing suit she bought used from that church rummage sale last year. She didn't want to look like a sex magnet in that bathing suit and it would make her mad I was telling you this, but Onora was and always will be a strong shot of sex magnet. Those bare thighs reflecting the cheesy sunset purple, my god. Hold your breath, why don't you?

Edie was having an off summer. You know how cruel adolescence can be. It was mostly the lack of laughing that concerned me. She used to have one of those big laughs where it almost sounds made up, like she's pretending, but she isn't. It's real and then when it's gone you don't know how to be around her. She felt lower to the ground somehow, like one of those five-lined skinks, those little lizards with the blue tails, hiding in the grass at our feet, but soon the sky would save her.

And Belle was the first one to break the silence that had come over us. She was always the first to recognize we were heading too far into sentimental land, and she righted the course, sent us back to irony.

Post Alice: Scene 1 – Sunset

BELLE: (*in her own space and time*) It's so fucking beautiful. What a bitch of a sunset.

ONORA, EDIE, and WENLOCK laugh.

WENLOCK: Yeah. She really said that. "What a bitch of a sunset." And that became gold, you know. A thing we said whenever we could. Always. We just threw it in whenever and that was it, we would die laughing. If you got straight A's – what a bitch of a sunset. If your steamy crush liked you back – what a bitch of a sunset. If you got into that fancy Paris film school you applied to –

BELLE: What. A. Bitch.

Dirt bike revving heard by all the women. All affected in their own ways.

WENLOCK: It was the best line to use, especially if things got too real, too ...

The following song is sung in the round, starting with BELLE. The last to join is WENLOCK.

ALL: (*singing*) Fire's Burning
Fire's Burning
Draw Nearer
Draw Nearer
In the glowing
In the glowing
What a bitch of a sunset.

BELLE hits her thumb with her knife. WENLOCK feels it, too.

BELLE: Oh!

BELLE puts her thumb in her mouth and searches around for something to wrap it with. WENLOCK, ONORA, and EDIE exit.

SCENE 2
BLEEDING

Continued from the last scene. BELLE is trying to stop her finger from bleeding.

BELLE: Jesus Christ.

ONORA enters. She is now in the same space and time as BELLE.

ONORA: (*unaware of Belle's cut*) There she is.

BELLE: Onora.

ONORA: Our little Cowbell.

BELLE: No. Onora. You're early.

ONORA: Our little Cowbell in a blanket by the fire.

BELLE: Just gimme a minute, I gotta –

ONORA: Are you okay?

BELLE: No, I'm fine, I just –

ONORA: What?

BELLE: It's nothing.

ONORA: Your thumb. Oh my god.

BELLE: It's worse than it looks. It's fine.

ONORA: A cut! You can't have a cut.

BELLE: No. It's okay.

ONORA: You can't have a cut in your condition.

BELLE: In my condition?

ONORA: Do I need to get you to the hospital?

BELLE: It's just a cut. Onora, I'm fine.

ONORA: Shit. Shit.

BELLE: Calm down.

ONORA: Shit.

BELLE: Look. (*opening the wrapping to show that she's fine*) See.
It's not even bleeding anymore.

ONORA: It's not bleeding.

BELLE: No big deal.

> *ONORA realizes she is overreacting. ONORA and BELLE*
> *laugh together for a moment.*

ONORA: Belle, I –

BELLE: This is exactly what I didn't want. You all coming here
with those dingbat eyes looking at me like that.

ONORA: I know.

BELLE: Screw off with those eyes, Onora.

ONORA: Sorry.

BELLE: And you're early. You had to come early.

ONORA: It's not that early.

BELLE: It feels early.

ONORA: I mean, I can go if you need some time or –

BELLE: Onora.

ONORA: Cowbell.

BELLE: What else?

ONORA: What?

BELLE: With you, dingbat eyes. There's something else with you.

ONORA: There is?

BELLE: Oh hell, yes. I know those stupid eyes aren't just for
    pathetic little me.

ONORA: No. What? Nothing.

BELLE: Well, that was convincing.

ONORA: Yeah.

BELLE: You know you can tell him to stop.

ONORA: It's not what you think.

BELLE: He's putting you under too much pressure. If you don't
    want more to do, tell your dad not to give you any more
    properties to manage, O. He's going to end up giving them all to
    you someday and just, like, fly off to Belize or something with
    that hot mom of yours.

ONORA: He's – he's just looking out for me.

BELLE: Tell him if it's too much.

ONORA: It's not, I, uh –

BELLE: What?

ONORA: Well, actually, I think he's coming into focus a little better these days, my dad. I'm seeing him more clearly, maybe.

BELLE: Oh. Oh, wait. Did he finally talk to you?

ONORA: Uh. Not exactly.

BELLE: Holy shit.

ONORA: I really didn't want to bring this up today, Cowbell. I mean with you and the, well, news, and my life is clearly not why we're here –

BELLE: Onora.

ONORA: Okay.

> ONORA *takes a deep breath and looks directly at the audience, letting them know she can see them to implicate them in her story. BELLE listens to ONORA as if she's telling her this.*

ONORA: She's good, isn't she? Sensing me out like that. Belle knows I've been researching into my dad's family because he never talks about them. I asked growing up, of course, who doesn't want to know the truth about your family? Meet them, maybe? But he only offered half-answers. I guess he just couldn't face it yet, his whole family ripping apart because of something about his sister.

When I couldn't get answers out of my dad, I started my own search. I even went to this archive in Ottawa once, scoured census data for his name, our name. But the only kind of breakthrough was last week when I went to visit this community, mostly Haudenosaunee. I heard Dad say the name of the area once in the kitchen when he thought I wasn't listening, but I was listening.

Without telling him, I just got in the car. On the highway, you know, where the rocks start to take over the sides of the road, I was wondering what the fuck I was even doing and after a while stopped in this little gas station, maybe fifteen minutes from where I was going, because the tears in my eyes were making it too difficult to see the road. I was so frustrated. Like, what did I think I was going to do when I got there, start knocking on doors?

And then this guy in a pickup truck pulled up beside me and yelled out the window, "Do I know you?" and I said no, and he said, "No, I know you," and he asked me who my father was. "Oh yeah. I know you." I was trying to find the words to ask him what he knew about me, because this stranger in a pickup truck clearly knew more about who I was than I did. But he didn't offer anything more than that and drove away. I know you.

    ONORA takes out a letter.

And then today this letter came. I think this is from my grandmother.

BELLE: You have a new grandmother. Holy shit, Onora, that's amazing.

ONORA: It's something.

BELLE: Oh, you got the dream, a whole new family, a new identity. A new reason to stay alive in this fucked-up world.

ONORA: Okay.

BELLE: This is so cool. I mean, so it's confirmed now, right? You can stop waiting for your dad to tell you the obvious. You are Indigenous.

ONORA: Well. I'm – I mean, am I?

BELLE: Well, your dad is, his mom is. And so you are. That's kind of how it works, isn't it?

ONORA: I honestly don't know. I think technically it's supposed to be my mother, maybe. And I think there's a lot of politics behind that, too, that I need to research more about, and well, I really don't know anything. I mean, I haven't even opened the letter yet.

BELLE: You haven't?

ONORA: I haven't.

BELLE: The letter with all the answers to your family secrets. You haven't opened it yet?

ONORA: No. I'm just, I'm having a little trouble actually getting the envelope open, I guess.

BELLE: Well hey, I can certainly help you with that.

BELLE tries aggressively to help ONORA open the letter.

ONORA: Oh. Uh –

BELLE: Give it to me. I'll rip her open. Let's see what this long-lost family has got to say.

ONORA: Belle, that is kind, very kind, but I'm just, well I'm – oh my god. Your finger.

BELLE: What?

ONORA: That finger is still bleeding.

BELLE: Oh no, Onora –

ONORA: I'm going to get you a real Band-Aid.

BELLE: It's really fine.

ONORA: Just give me a minute. No trouble. Do you have any in the bathroom?

BELLE: Maybe. I don't know.

ONORA: I'll look.

BELLE: The kitchen, maybe. And don't give me those dingbat eyes.

ONORA: Just stay here.

> *ONORA exits.*

SCENE 3
INCOMING

Continued from the last scene. Seated at the fire, BELLE sees a plane in the sky right above her.

BELLE: What the ...?

BELLE realizes the plane is coming in to land on her field.

BELLE: You're kidding me. Onora! Onora, come see this! You're not going to believe it.

BELLE watches the plane prepare to land.

BELLE: You little fucker. You better not crash in my field. Onora!

ONORA enters with a first-aid kit.

ONORA: What? Are you okay?

BELLE: Look.

ONORA: Oh lord. I mean, I knew she was going to fly in, but not *fly in*, fly in.

BELLE: You knew about this?

ONORA: Not this, Belle. Come on. This is all Edie.

BELLE: She better not smash into my barn and die on my property.

ONORA: This is so dangerous.

BELLE and ONORA: (*making a sound mimicking the landing of the plane*) Eeeeeeeeh.

ONORA: Oh my god.

When the plane safely lands, BELLE and ONORA cheer and clap.

BELLE and ONORA: Yeah!

BELLE: Edie! You are a nightmare! No trespassing! Get off my property!

EDIE and WENLOCK enter.

EDIE: Special delivery!

WENLOCK: Hey, Sis!

BELLE: You little jerk. What are you doing here?

WENLOCK: I knew you'd be happy to see me. Surprised?

BELLE: Ah, yeah.

ONORA: I wouldn't be surprised if the neighbours are calling the cops right now.

WENLOCK and ONORA see each other for the first time in years. Subtle fireworks between them.

WENLOCK: Hey, Onora.

ONORA: Heya, Wen.

WENLOCK: You look good.

ONORA: Oh. I, uh –

BELLE: Yeah. I just noticed you look kinda dressed up.

ONORA: Me? No. This is just nothing.

EDIE: What's with the first-aid kit?

BELLE: Oh, uh –

EDIE: Did something happen?

ONORA: No. Well, not really, just a cut.

WENLOCK: A cut on who? You?

BELLE: It's just my thumb.

WENLOCK: Shit.

EDIE: Oh boy.

BELLE: It's fine, really.

WENLOCK: Should we go to the hospital?

ONORA: That's what I said.

BELLE: No.

WENLOCK: No? Just no?

BELLE: I'm fine.

WENLOCK: Of course you are.

BELLE: I am. And we're gonna sit here and have a nice time. That's
    why you got the fancy fly-in entrance, isn't it?

WENLOCK: I guess, but if you hurt yourself ...

BELLE: I'm fine, I said.

EDIE: Let me see that thing.

> BELLE shows EDIE the cut.

EDIE: Yeah. Fine.

WENLOCK: Really?

EDIE: She's got worse cuts coming to her.

ONORA: Edie!

EDIE: It's the truth, isn't it?

BELLE: It's the truth.

> BELLE mimes getting her leg cut off and laughs, but no
> one else does. EDIE grabs the first-aid kit and dumps
> some stuff out.

ONORA: Oh. I was going to …

EDIE: I got it. Call it professional courtesy.

ONORA: Okay.

> EDIE takes BELLE's hand, wipes it with an alcohol swab,
> and puts on a Band-Aid.

BELLE: See, it's fine.

WENLOCK: I see.

BELLE: Sit down. Can we sit down now?

> WENLOCK sits.

BELLE: And drink.

> BELLE hands WENLOCK a beer.

WENLOCK: Oh, I'm – thanks.

BELLE: Drink.

BELLE hands out other beers. Revving can be heard far in the background. Backs stiffen.

ONORA: (*to WENLOCK so only she can hear*) It's okay. He's not here. You can drink.

WENLOCK drinks but looks over her shoulder.

ONORA: (*to the audience*) Forgot about the letter? Still thinking about it? She definitely is. Belle didn't like my dingbat eyes earlier, but it's her eyes that are the dangerous ones right now. They are telling me she wants to pin me down and rip open the envelope. Steal my feelings. Give me a minute, Cowbell. I thought telling you would release some of my feelings back into my body, but nothing yet.

SCENE 4 ·
GOOD NEWS

Continued from the last scene.

EDIE: Hey now, I feel cheated. I was promised a fire.

ONORA: I was getting to it.

EDIE: Well, get to it then.

BELLE: What? You don't see it?

EDIE: See what?

BELLE: The fire.

> *BELLE, EDIE, ONORA, and WENLOCK stare into the firepit for a second.*

ONORA: Belle, I, uh …

BELLE: Oh my god.

> *BELLE starts to laugh.*

ONORA: Cowbell.

EDIE: She got you.

WENLOCK: And you.

BELLE: I think I got you too, you little shit. Jesus. The cancer's not in my eyeballs.

> *EDIE starts to laugh. WENLOCK and ONORA look at each other.*

EDIE: Not in your eyeballs, Jesus.

BELLE: Here, I'll make the fire.

ONORA: Oh. I don't mind.

BELLE: Relax. I got it.

> *BELLE starts to make the fire.*

BELLE: Wait. Edie. What the fuck?

EDIE: What the fuck yourself.

BELLE: You didn't bring along the best part of you. You were promised a fire and I think I was promised a Chris.

EDIE: You want a kiss?

BELLE: A Chris. Your Chris.

EDIE: I'm very good at kisses.

BELLE: Please no. Edie, I refuse your kisses.

> *EDIE ignores this and gives BELLE a friendly kiss.*

EDIE: Chris, he kinda thought this should be an us-four kinda thing, and I think he thought kinda right. Plus, he got a last-minute flight, so ... sends his love, though.

WENLOCK: You two looked so happy together when I got there.

ONORA: They're adorable.

WENLOCK: Your married-couple banter is the right kind of cute.

ONORA: Not annoying at all. Impressive, really.

EDIE: He's okay I guess, for a husband.

BELLE: I don't know how he puts up with you.

EDIE: Okay, now. You all should be happy because you pretty little things get all of me today.

BELLE: Lucky us.

ONORA: I think so.

WENLOCK: That sounds like good news to me.

EDIE: Oh, hey Wen, here we go, tell them your good news. This is nuts. She was talking about it on the whole flight over here.

WENLOCK: Oh. Uh. Sure. Yeah.

ONORA: Good news? I love good news.

EDIE: Listen to this.

WENLOCK: Well, yeah. I was asked to write and direct a feature.

ONORA: Oh my god!

EDIE: Great, eh?

BELLE: Very great.

WENLOCK: Now, it's not for sure. And there's a lot of red tape to get through and funding, all that bullshit, but yeah. It just might happen.

EDIE: Oh, it'll happen. I always knew you were going to do incredible things, kiddo.

ONORA: That's so exciting. Congrats. I watched that other one of yours, the uh – *The Marble Wine*?

WENLOCK: You watched that?

ONORA: Of course I watched it. Belle did a showing at the library.

WENLOCK: She did?

BELLE: Don't say I don't do anything for you.

ONORA: I loved it.

EDIE: Me too. Short and sweet.

WENLOCK: Well, it was a short film, so –

EDIE: Exactly. The best kind.

WENLOCK: I'm glad you liked it.

ONORA: I loved the part where the woman was riding the tractor topless through the vineyard.

WENLOCK: Yeah?

ONORA: It was cool how you juxtaposed that with the skyscraper in the next shot. Gorgeous.

BELLE: We got ourselves a film critic over here.

ONORA: I mean, I don't know anything about film, but I liked that.

WENLOCK: Thank you. That really means a lot to me. I fought for that shot with my team for a while. None of them got it until I made them do it and then they were like, okay. Maybe she knows what she's doing.

EDIE: Yeah, you do.

ONORA: Clearly. If someone wants you to make a feature.

WENLOCK: Well, actually, Onora, you might be able to help me with that.

ONORA: Me? Help the big-shot director?

BELLE: She's just Wenlock.

WENLOCK: Yeah. I mean you might all be able to help me. The story for the film is actually inspired by the Mistie Murray case.

BELLE: What?

EDIE: You didn't say that.

WENLOCK: Yeah. You remember how into that story we all were?

ONORA: Into it? More like obsessed. You know what, I think I still have our old scrapbooks full of news articles and, like, a hundred of those missing-person posters somewhere in the attic.

WENLOCK: Oh wow. Do you think I could maybe look through those?

ONORA: Come over any time.

EDIE: What did we call ourselves again?

WENLOCK: I was trying to think of it the other day.

ONORA: There were a lot of *M*'s.

WENLOCK: The Mistie something Association?

EDIE: Club. I remember club was in it.

BELLE: MMMC. The Mistie Murray Mystery Club. It's really not that complicated.

EDIE: Mystery Club. What a bunch of dorks.

WENLOCK: Remember when we had a seance in this backyard trying to communicate with her?

BELLE: I do. You made me dig up our entire herb garden to light on fire. Mom was pretty pissed about that.

ONORA: We were so convinced she would speak to us because we were girls from the area too. That we were connected somehow.

EDIE: Think it might still work?

ONORA: What? A seance?

EDIE: It's worth a shot.

WENLOCK: Yes, please.

BELLE: Oh god, no.

ONORA: I think we might have to for research, that's what you call this kinda thing, research, right Wenlock?

WENLOCK: I could swing a seance as research.

BELLE: And pay us all? I could use some of that movie money.

EDIE: You're gonna make your baby sister pay you to participate in a little backyard fun?

BELLE: You think calling on the dead sounds like fun?

EDIE: You know it.

WENLOCK: How do we start?

ONORA: I remember there was chanting involved.

WENLOCK: Chanting for sure. And then the herb fire?

BELLE: Nobody is burning my herbs. I finally got Mom's garden back to its former glory.

EDIE: Oh wait! How about pot? We could burn that.

WENLOCK: That might work.

ONORA: Sounds good to me.

> *EDIE gets a joint out of her pocket and lights it up.*

EDIE: You guys get the chanting going.

WENLOCK and ONORA: Oooh, aaaah.

BELLE: Have you ever chanted before?

WENLOCK: I thought that was pretty good.

BELLE: It sounded more like you saw a double rainbow in the sky or something, not, you know, bringing dead-girl spirits back from the grave.

EDIE: I think maybe it will help if you say something in the chant.

WENLOCK: Okay. Okay. I got it. In the flames. In the waves. In the sky. In the earth.

EDIE: Yeah. That sounds good.

> *EDIE starts making a chanting noise and sustains it while others speak.*

WENLOCK and ONORA: In the flames. In the waves. In the sky. In the earth.

ONORA: Join in, Cowbell.

BELLE: I'm good.

WENLOCK and ONORA: In the flames. In the waves. In the sky. In the earth.

WENLOCK: Mistie, can you hear me? We are calling on Mistie. Can you hear me? Mistie.

BELLE: Stop that. Please.

ONORA: Mistie. Hello, Mistie.

BELLE: Jesus.

EDIE: Mistie, we want to hear from Mistie.

BELLE: You too? Really?

EDIE: Shhh.

>   *Pause. Sound of a loud crack in the distance.*

ONORA: Oh god.

BELLE: She's kidding, Mistie. Please don't show yourself.

EDIE: We got enough shit going on here.

>   *ALL laugh, except maybe BELLE.*

EDIE: That was genuinely kinda freaky.

ONORA: (*to WENLOCK*) Look at the goosebumps on your arm.

WENLOCK: I'm gonna have to work this in, to the film, I mean.

BELLE: You know, Miss Director, you're not the only one with good news these days.

ONORA: (*to the audience*) Oh no.

WENLOCK: I didn't think I was.

ONORA: (*to the audience*) Give me a minute, Cowbell.

EDIE: Great. Let's keep this good-news train rolling.

ONORA: (*to the audience*) I'm not ready yet.

BELLE: Onora's got something exciting going on, too.

ONORA: (*to the audience*) Here we go.

EDIE: Did you find Mistie Murray?

ONORA: What? No, no, no.

WENLOCK: What's your news?

ONORA: Well –

BELLE: It's big.

EDIE: (*to BELLE*) Okay. Everything's a competition with you.

BELLE: Tell them.

ONORA: Uh. Okay. My dad's mom, the one I didn't know existed, well, she wrote me a letter.

EDIE: Whoa.

WENLOCK: What?

BELLE: And?

EDIE: And?

ONORA: And I haven't opened it yet.

BELLE: But ...

ONORA: But it might tell me what happened with my dad and his family and why he never talks about being Haudenosaunee.

EDIE: What? Seriously?

BELLE: Pretty big, eh?

WENLOCK: Extremely big. Are you okay?

ONORA: I honestly don't know.

BELLE: Show them the letter.

ONORA shows them the envelope.

EDIE: I'm sorry, but holy shit, like, how did I not know about this?

ONORA: Look, I just got this letter today, so.

WENLOCK: Today? As in, today?

ONORA: Yeah, just a couple hours ago. Dad doesn't even know about it.

EDIE: Wild.

WENLOCK: Are you sure you want to talk about this?

ONORA: I mean, it's a lot to process, clearly.

BELLE: It's so awesome.

EDIE: But Onora, you're like ...

ONORA: What?

EDIE: I mean, you're not really, I mean, you're like you.

ONORA: I am me, yes.

EDIE: Sorry, I mean, well, you know. Come on, you know what I mean, guys.

WENLOCK: What do you mean, Edie?

EDIE: I don't know. Sorry. Nothing.

ONORA: No, I'm sorry, Edie. I think I'm just not understanding.

EDIE: It's just that you're so ...

BELLE: White?

EDIE: Uh.

BELLE: Rich?

WENLOCK: Oh.

EDIE: No.

ONORA: No?

EDIE: I mean, I don't know.

ONORA: Oh, well. I, uh –

BELLE: Fucking racist, Edie.

EDIE: No. I mean, come on. That's just, shit.

BELLE: Racist.

EDIE: I'm not – I mean, I didn't mean to. Jesus. Onora, I'm sorry if I –

ONORA: No, no, no. I mean, clearly all people are complex and more than stereotypes, but I'm as confused about all this as you are.

EDIE: Yeah?

ONORA: I grew up with you guys, I'm like, I don't know.

BELLE: So you learn now and you embrace who you are.

WENLOCK: Who she is? Who is she, B?

ONORA: There's a lot for everyone to process, I guess.

BELLE: But you don't even know what you're processing without opening that letter.

WENLOCK: Which is hers, not ours, her story.

BELLE: It's more than a story. It's her life.

WENLOCK: I know that.

ONORA: Guys.

BELLE: Life goes on without you, Wen. We're not just stories for you to dig up whenever you feel like being a tourist in your hometown again.

WENLOCK: I don't think that.

BELLE: Some of us actually still live here.

ONORA: Maybe we should just relax. Belle, you especially –

BELLE: Me especially?

ONORA: Well, yeah, with your condition.

EDIE: Guys.

BELLE: Stop with the fucking condition already. I'm fine.

ONORA: Sorry. I know, I just –

WENLOCK: We're here five minutes, and you're already pushing us away.

EDIE: (*loudly*) Hey dorks!

    ALL stop fighting.

BELLE: What?

EDIE: Onora, I think you're right, I think I am racist.

ONORA: Oh.

BELLE: Well, yeah.

WENLOCK: I don't think she actually said you're racist, Edie.

BELLE: I did.

EDIE: But like, I think I must be. I didn't know any Indigenous people lived around here. Oh, I didn't know your father was Haudenosaunee? I swear to god.

ONORA: I know.

BELLE: But you must have known Mistie was –

EDIE: No.

BELLE: No?

EDIE: Absolutely no. Really?

WENLOCK: Really.

EDIE: I mean, how did I not know that? This is what I mean. Look, I remember learning about Louis Riel in elementary school, I guess, but that's in, like, Winnipeg or something, not that Indigenous people lived here, in our community. Of course they live here, they must live everywhere. How stupid am I?

ONORA: You're not stupid.

BELLE: That's colonialism.

EDIE: Yeah. Yeah, I guess, right? It's wild. We had poor Mistie's face plastered on the news and on posters, but I had no idea. I just thought she was a white girl like us, or like me, I guess. Sorry, Jesus. What is wrong with me? Like, there must have been other Indigenous women missing, too. There's that national inquiry and stuff now, right? Were they ... I mean, they must have been disappearing at the same time as Mistie, right?

ONORA: And before Mistie.

BELLE: And after Mistie.

EDIE: Do you remember hearing about them growing up?

WENLOCK: No. I don't.

BELLE: Yeah. No. Nothing.

EDIE: Yeah. Did you, Onora? I mean, I guess you must have?

ONORA: Um. Yeah. A bit. (*to the audience*) What I want to tell them is no, actually, not really. Not really at all. Growing up nobody told me anything. My dad didn't tell me about his own family, how is he going to bring up something like Missing and Murdered Indigenous Women and Girls? I mean, what I really want to tell them is that this might be part of my family's story, too, might be what I find in this letter, might be what happened to his sister, my aunt, but no, the truth is I don't know. Oh, look at that, there's an emotion filling that vacant body of mine. Anger. Not the one I was expecting.

The fire's flames spark up.

EDIE: (*singing beautifully*) In the flames. In the waves. In the sky. In the earth.

SCENE 5
LOST GIRLS

Out of the space and time of the last scene. This scene does not feel as though it actually happened, but is more the subtext of the play, a sort of haunting. ONORA takes a red cloth and hangs it like a dress – evoking the REDress project.

ALL join in a song. Beautiful, earnest a capella harmony unaccompanied or lightly accompanied by traditionally Celtic instruments.

ALL:
(*singing*) In the flames. In the waves. In the sky. In the earth.
Digging holes in the town hall.
Where do our lost girls go?

Phantom birds flying through the atmosphere.
Soft strands among the trees.
Where do our lost girls go?

Awake among the flames, hot breath in your dreams.
A thick fog hides the smoke.
Where do our lost girls go?

Women wash red linens in the cold of the lake.
Feet caught in the undertow.
Where do our lost girls go?

In the roots of the willow tree grow teeth and fingernails.
Unearth the smell of dirt.
Where do our lost girls go?

In the flames. In the waves. In the sky. In the earth.
Digging holes in the town hall.
Where do our lost girls go?

SCENE 6
PHANTOM LIMB

Coming out of the trance from the last scene. EDIE takes a big swig of her beer and gets up.

EDIE: You got more wood around here, Cowbell?

BELLE: Oh, uh. Maybe down by the road?

EDIE: Wouldn't it make more sense to have it here by the fire?

BELLE: Yeah. probably.

EDIE: If I go to the road, I'm not going to find any wood, am I?

BELLE: Not exactly. Lots of old dead trees, though, and an axe.

EDIE: So how are we supposed to keep this friend that you just started here?

BELLE: What? You didn't bring a bushel of wood with you?

EDIE: In my plane?

BELLE: Yeah. After saving those lives or whatever good deed you were doing in that aircraft parked on my lawn, you didn't think of packing a little wood like a good neighbour?

EDIE: What's that beside you there?

BELLE: Where?

EDIE: I see wood. Do you see wood, Wen?

WENLOCK: Yup.

BELLE: That's not wood.

EDIE: No? I think it's wood. Do you see wood, Onora?

ONORA: I see wood.

EDIE: She sees –

BELLE: Please stop saying "wood."

EDIE: Wood.

BELLE: Well, you can't have this.

EDIE: No? So there's no wood except for the wood sitting beside you, and we can't use it.

BELLE: That's right.

EDIE: Is it special?

BELLE: Please don't.

EDIE picks up the wooden leg.

EDIE: Oh my, this is special. It looks like a little art project going on here.

ONORA: Whoa.

WENLOCK: Edie, that's um. That's a ...

EDIE: What? What is it?

WENLOCK: Well, that's a leg.

EDIE: Leg? Is this a leg?

BELLE: It's a leg.

EDIE: (*pointing at BELLE's leg*) For your?

BELLE: Obviously not. How could that be for my ...

EDIE: Okay.

ONORA: Guys, maybe we should put that down.

EDIE: Down where? In the fire? If it's not anything special, we could just –

BELLE: No!

ONORA: Edie.

WENLOCK: Maybe that's enough, she looks like she wants it back.

EDIE: Oh, so it is precious. This is a precious artifact. My apologies. Here.

EDIE pretends to give BELLE her leg back.

BELLE: Thank you ... Okay.

ONORA: Oh.

EDIE: If you want it back, you gotta tell us. What's the deal? What did the doctor say?

BELLE: I don't know. I'm fine. It's fine.

WENLOCK: Fine?

BELLE: It's just a leg. It's a leg, and they say when it's gone, all is gone.

WENLOCK: What?

ONORA: Oh my god.

BELLE: No. I mean, once the leg is gone the cancer is gone, they think.

EDIE: Well fuck, that's good. Right?

ONORA: Really good.

WENLOCK: You have a cure.

BELLE: Just a little hack job to this little lady here and wham! Gone. Bye-bye cancer.

EDIE: (*giving the leg back to BELLE*) Here.

BELLE: It's stupid. I know.

ONORA: It's very well whittled. The doctor might let you use part of it for the, uh – replacement.

BELLE: I'm pretty sure the doctor would frown on me making my own leg, O. What is this, the Middle Ages? It's just … I'm getting used to the idea now that it's going to be me and my leg together alone in this old house all day and all night from now on. I'm sure you all noticed Jackson's absence by now.

EDIE: How long's it been this time?

BELLE: Long enough. He knew I shouldn't have gone to this latest doctor. He told me it would be bad news. He knew. He's out dealing with it somewhere.

WENLOCK: He should be dealing with it with you.

ONORA: Wen.

BELLE: But I got you little nosy jerks to help me with that, right? I mean, finally you had to fly in to see me when you thought I might be dying. Well, I'm not. I'm fine. It'll be fine. Don't worry, you can go back to your life tomorrow.

WENLOCK: I can stay the week.

BELLE: Oh, a week. Well, fuck me.

WENLOCK: Unless you're busy with work or something.

BELLE: Work? No, not this girl.

ONORA: You're taking a break from the library? That's good.

BELLE: A break, yeah.

EDIE: It's not a break.

BELLE: Ding, ding, ding, Edie's right, yup, the library let me go
when I got the news.

ONORA: What?

EDIE: Because of your leg?

BELLE: Yes.

WENLOCK: You're kidding me.

EDIE: Tell me who needs a beating.

BELLE: And. Because of my leg and I might have tried to teach
some kids how to use a knife at storytime.

WENLOCK: Wait, what?

EDIE: That's an important skill.

ONORA: You didn't.

BELLE: I had just got the news about the big C and started this guy,
and things had been slow at work, so after a morning whittle I
brought it along with me to, maybe, you know, pass the time. It's

been, uh, soothing I guess. And there's this regular group of kids at storytime who I've gotten to know pretty well. Most of them are little shitheads, and I love them. We sat down to read *The Secret Garden* and, well, even though I usually love that story with the pigheaded girl who finally finds love with all the magical growing things everywhere, I just, I couldn't. I asked if the kids were cool if we skipped right to the craft, and the smart little jerks started asking what was wrong. Nobody had asked me that yet, but they knew. And then one asked about the leg I brought along, so I told them about my cancer and showed them the leg I was making. It's kinda a craft, right? It was actually a really beautiful moment, you know, me and the kids and the leg. We were crying together, and I was showing them the different designs and how to make them. Then their parents showed up and well, yeah, I guess it looked a little weird with all the kids bawling their little faces off and me holding a knife. So yes. I was fired because of my leg, but the library would probably say it was child endangerment or something.

Beat.

EDIE: Do you guys see it?

ONORA: See what?

EDIE: I think we might got one.

WENLOCK: Oh. Yeah. I see it now.

ONORA: What am I missing?

EDIE: You don't see it, O? It's just right over there. What a ...

ALL: Bitch of a sunset.

EDIE: Are there really dead trees in the front there, B?

BELLE: Oh there's tons of them, still got some of the old ash.

EDIE: I'll be back.

EDIE exits.

SCENE 7
PINK TIGER-STRIPED BATHING SUIT

Continued from the previous scene.

WENLOCK: You were always the best with the long stories, you know. You did all the voices and knew where to put the emphasis. Way better than Mom was and Dad even, and he wasn't half bad with the stories.

BELLE: He was a good liar, wasn't he?

WENLOCK: I guess we all are.

BELLE: And Jackson too.

Beat.

BELLE: You know, Wen, I've been whittling this leg and thinking.

Revving starts in the background and gets louder.

WENLOCK: Thinking.

BELLE: Yeah. Thinking. I'm obviously going to be fine, but I'm realizing like, uh, time is not what I thought it was, maybe.

WENLOCK: Okay.

BELLE: So I, uh, well, we never really talked about that night with the bitch of a sunset and that party at the motel Jackson brought us to, so if you want to ...

The revving stops.

WENLOCK: The house looks different.

BELLE: New roof this year.

WENLOCK: Like, like a calf.

BELLE: The roof?

WENLOCK: Like the back of a calf.

BELLE: Yeah. I see that.

ONORA: (*to the audience*) Doesn't look much like a calf to me. While they avoid talking about osteosarcoma and Jackson Maynard, I'm caught thinking about all the conversations my dad avoided having with me. All the times he could have told me about what's in this letter lighting a fire in my pocket.

And you know that conversation, the one I wasn't ready for earlier? Well, it probably won't come up again tonight. Everyone just wants to let everything go. Unfinished. Unresolved.

WENLOCK: O?

ONORA: Yeah.

WENLOCK: Sorry, did you say something?

ONORA: I don't know, did I?

BELLE: I'm gonna grab some more beer.

ONORA: You should eat something, Cowbell.

BELLE: Yeah. Okay. I suppose you're all hungry at this point, eh? I'll dig up something and maybe find an old chair to burn, too.

> *BELLE exits.*

WENLOCK: O, you know you don't have to stay here. I mean, I know you have a little reading and a shit ton of processing to do and you might be understandably distracted.

ONORA: And leave this very fun time we're having helping your sister through her bone cancer?

WENLOCK: Yeah. You do not have to stay.

ONORA: I don't want to leave.

WENLOCK: Good. I mean, I'm glad you're here.

ONORA: Oh yeah?

WENLOCK: For Belle, yeah. She needs you. Clearly.

ONORA: Right.

WENLOCK: And ... me.

ONORA: And you?

WENLOCK: I'm – you remember that pink tiger-striped bathing suit you got once at that church rummage sale?

ONORA: The one from high school?

WENLOCK: The one from high school.

ONORA: I do.

WENLOCK: Well, I had a memory of you in it the other day.

ONORA: You had a memory of me in a pink tiger-striped bathing suit.

WENLOCK: Yes.

ONORA: A good memory?

WENLOCK: A great memory.

ONORA: I see.

WENLOCK: And now I'm realizing that is a very weird thing to tell you right now and –

ONORA and WENLOCK kiss.

ONORA: I'm sorry.

WENLOCK: No. I'm sorry. I was talking about you in a bathing suit in high school.

ONORA: Yeah. That was all on you.

ONORA and WENLOCK kiss again.

WENLOCK: And that one? Was that on me, too?

ONORA: I think it was, yeah.

WENLOCK: Fair enough. Shit, Onora. Hi.

ONORA: Hi. It's been a while.

WENLOCK: A little while, yeah. You know, I've been thinking about other things than just bathing suits.

ONORA: Like staying?

WENLOCK: Where? Here?

ONORA: For your sister. She clearly needs you.

WENLOCK: My sister doesn't need me.

ONORA: Wen.

WENLOCK: She's Cowbell. Come on, she doesn't need anybody.

ONORA: She's more fragile than you might think.

WENLOCK: Fragile? For fuck's sake.

ONORA: She has cancer, Wen.

WENLOCK: And I have my movie. I can't just – you want me to give up that shot?

ONORA: No. No. Of course not.

EDIE enters dragging a whole tree.

EDIE: Ta-dah. I'd like to see your sister try to whittle this.

WENLOCK: Well, that's impressive.

ONORA: I'm going to go help Belle in the kitchen.

ONORA exits. EDIE cuts off a part of the tree and adds it to the fire.

EDIE: Everything okay there?

WENLOCK: Why wouldn't it be?

EDIE: Look. You know it's okay, right?

WENLOCK: What?

EDIE: You don't have to hide anything from me. You two. I mean, you weren't that good at hiding it anyway. I get why you felt you needed to hide it maybe in the rural nineties, but why now? Who cares?

WENLOCK: Does Belle know?

EDIE: Love is a powerful emotion, hard to keep inside.

WENLOCK: I think Onora just asked me to stay.

EDIE: So stay.

WENLOCK: But I –

EDIE: Or don't, I don't know. I'm gonna see if I can find another one of these before it gets too dark and I get too drunk to swing this friend around.

>   *EDIE exits.*

SCENE 8
THE PITCH

WENLOCK is alone on stage in a different time and space.

WENLOCK: (*to the audience*) Yes. Thank you. I appreciate the chance to talk to you all today. I've been a fan of the films your company makes for a long time now, their raw-yet-ethereal quality. It's an honour to be talking to you about my proposed film, *The Mysterious Case of Mistie Murray*.

Mistie Murray was sixteen years old when she went missing May 31st, 1995, from the small Lake Huron community of Goderich, Ontario. On that seemingly normal day, she got up, told her parents she would be late after school because of band practice, and went to her usual high school classes. At one point she visited the school nurse for an undisclosed reason. Later, around 3 p.m., she tried to call her mother at work but couldn't get through. It turns out Mistie didn't have band practice after school that day and she never made her way home.

EDIE enters with some wood and tends to the fire throughout the rest of the scene.

WENLOCK: (*to the audience*) It's a sort of documentary, yes, but also fiction, well, more transparently fiction than the usual documentary, a blending of fact and fiction. Did you get a chance to see my last film I sent in, *The Marble Wine*? Oh yeah? Thank you. Those same tone and style choices. The ones that play with the real and unreal, that's part of the vision of this project, too. I mean, that's the horrific truth about a mystery like this, isn't it? There are many versions of the truth depending on who you ask, and I'm interested in playing out the possibilities of what happened to Mistie Murray as if they could all be true and fiction at the same time.

ONORA and BELLE enter with food, beer, and the library supply box.

WENLOCK: (*to the audience*) But really I want to focus on who is still here, who is still alive and what happens to them. I think we all know a similar story. See this story – yes, I'm actually from the community and, well, it hung over us growing up, especially us girls from the area.

BELLE: (*in real time of the play, others hear*) Here we go. Yes. Here. And drink.

> *WENLOCK, EDIE, ONORA, and BELLE drink shots.*

ONORA: (*in real time of the play, others hear*) Oh my, my.

WENLOCK: (*in real time of the play, others hear*) Eeh!

EDIE: (*in real time of the play, others hear*) Yee-haw. What else do you have in that box there?

BELLE: (*in real time of the play, others hear*) Stolen goods!

ONORA: (*in real time of the play, others hear*) Cowbell!

BELLE: (*in real time of the play, others hear*) Trust me, O. I wasn't leaving the library without taking a few friends with me. I stole some puppets. And we got some John Irving and Thomas King and even a little Alice Munro.

EDIE: (*in real time of the play, others hear*) We're such a wild bunch, stealing puppets and library books.

BELLE: (*indicating the puppet show, in real time of the play, others hear*) Here, help me with this.

WENLOCK: (*to the audience*) Before she went missing? Yes. There's a story there, too. Lots to build from for the film. Her biological mother – yeah, she was adopted in 1983 after a couple of years in foster care. She's often described as a happy child, but once she became a teenager, I guess she had a hard time finding herself, or steadying herself, maybe.

Mistie, at the time she went missing when she was just sixteen, she had an adult boyfriend. Yes. That was generally uncommon, of course, but, well, it did happen. My sister, for example, she started dating her now husband when she was just fifteen and he was twenty-three. Yeah. It's, uh, I find it troubling looking back now, yes. No, uh, my mother died when we were in elementary school, and my father knew him, trained him in motocross racing, so no, I don't think he saw an issue with it.

Mistie, she reconnected with her biological mother about nine or so months before she disappeared, and she was actually supposed to spend the weekend with her when she vanished. The story goes she was having complex feelings about her relationship with her biological mother, as well … as I imagine most adopted kids would. It was reported that she was looking forward to this weekend with her, though. Mistie had a bag packed and two hundred dollars on her dresser that she left behind the day she never came home.

SCENE 9
SHADOW STORIES

*Continued from the previous scene. The shadow puppet
show, which includes a beach and a lake, is set up. Like the
song in scene 5, this scene can feel like it could not have
happened in real time and is instead the subtext of the play.
The shadow puppet of a girl, child 1, appears.*

BELLE: On a beach next to the lake stood a child of sixteen. In the
water she knew there was an adventure lurking, but not the
kind that made her want to jump in.

*A shadow-puppet monster, monster 1, pokes its head
out of the water. It would be great if it looked like a
five-lined skink.*

WENLOCK: (*as monster 1*) Child on the beach!

ONORA: (*as child 1*) Yes, monster in the lake?

WENLOCK: (*as monster 1*) Why are you waiting there? Don't you
want to come play with me?

ONORA: (*as child 1*) I don't know.

WENLOCK: (*as monster 1*) You're welcome to run the other way,
but this place, this waiting, you can't stay here.

BELLE: The child thought for a moment and then put her feet
in the water.

Child 1 puts her feet in the water.

ONORA: (*as child 1*) Is this far enough?

WENLOCK: (*as monster 1*) Not even close.

The child 1 shadow puppet walks into the water up to her waist.

ONORA: (*as child 1*) How's this?

WENLOCK: (*as monster 1*) Take a deep breath in and hold my hand.

A tentacle comes out of the water.

ONORA: (*as child 1*) That doesn't look like any hand I've ever seen.

Child 1 holds the monster's tentacle.

WENLOCK: (*as monster 1*) Ready? One, two, three!

Monster 1 launches itself on shore and child 1 into the water.

ONORA: (*as child 1*) Wait! You tricked me!

WENLOCK: (*as monster 1*) Thank you, child. I've been trying to find a way on land for many years, and you finally freed me.

ONORA: (*as child 1*) But I want to go back.

WENLOCK: (*as monster 1*) Hold on now. The next part might hurt a little.

BELLE: And just like that the child turned into a stone and floated to the bottom of the lake.

Child 1 turns into a stone and monster 1 on the shore turns into a man shadow puppet and exits.

ONORA: (*as child 1*) Hello? Is there someone there?

EDIE: (*as child 2*) Hello. Welcome to the bottom of the lake.

ONORA: (*as child 1*) Who said that?

EDIE: (*as child 2*) Me, right here.

ONORA: (*as child 1*) Little stone, you can talk, too?

EDIE: (*as child 2*) Are you a child? I'm a child, trapped as a stone.

ONORA: (*as child 1*) Me too!

EDIE: (*as child 2*) It's peaceful here in the water. Let it lull you to sleep.

ONORA: (*as child 1*) Sleep! I can't sleep. I need to get back to the shore.

EDIE: (*as child 2*) You won't make many friends.

ONORA: (*as child 1*) There's more of us?

EDIE: (*as child 2*) All lake stones are lost children.

BELLE: (*as child 3*) Quiet! I'm trying to sleep!

EDIE: (*as child 2*) See?

ONORA: (*as child 1*) Well, we must work together, then.

BELLE: (*as child 3*) What's she saying?

EDIE: (*as child 2*) She wants us to work together.

BELLE: (*as child 3*) To do what?

ONORA: (*as child 1*) To get to dry land. Wake up, child stones! Get up and wake your heads.

WENLOCK: (*as child 4*) Who's that?

EDIE: (*as child 2*) She's new.

BELLE: (*as child 3*) I want to go back to bed.

ONORA: (*as child 1*) Child stones, it's our time. It's our moment to be free. Climb on me, here. Let's see what together we can be.

The stone shadow puppets turn into monster 2.

EDIE: (*as child 2*) Look, it's a child!

BELLE: (*as child 3*) Let's get 'im!

ONORA: (*as child 1*) Just let me do all the talking.

Monster 2 floats to the surface.

ONORA: (*as child 1*) Child on the beach!

EDIE: (*as child 4*) Yes, monster in the lake?

ONORA: (*as child 1*) Why are you waiting there? Don't you want to come play with me?

EDIE: (*as child 4*) I don't know.

ONORA: (*as child 1*) You're welcome to run the other way, but this place, this waiting, you can't stay here.

BELLE: The child thought for a moment and then put her feet in the water.

Child 4 puts her feet in the water.

EDIE: (*as child 4*) Is this far enough?

ONORA: (*as child 1*) Not even close.

Child 4 walks into the water up to her waist.

EDIE: (*as child 4*) How's this?

ONORA: (*as child 1*) Take a deep breath in and hold my hand.

A tentacle comes out of the water.

EDIE: (*as child 4*) That doesn't look like any hand I've ever seen.

Child 4 holds the monster's tentacle. The man shadow puppet enters onto the beach.

WENLOCK: (*as monster 1*) Hèy! Wait! That's my child!

ONORA: Oh look, it's the man.

The man shadow puppet goes into the water to get his child.

WENLOCK: (*as monster 1*) Don't take my child.

ONORA: (*as child 1*) That was never the plan.

The tentacles wrap around the man shadow puppet, and child 4 runs to shore.

BELLE: Once in the monster's grasp, the man resumed his true form and the stone children of the lake made a great sacrifice that day.

ONORA: (*as child 1*) If we leave him, he might do it again.

BELLE: Each turned back to a stone and rested on his tentacles, on his head, on his heart until he fell down to the bottom.

ALL take apart the puppet show.

ALL: (*singing or chanting*) Stone children. Stone children. Keeping him down. Below the waves. Monsters in the lake.

SCENE 10
POST ALICE

WENLOCK is finishing her pitch.

WENLOCK: And opening image for the film? Fade in on four girls, around fifteen, sixteen. A few years after Mistie disappeared. The girls are running up to the top of the Goderich bluffs on Lake Huron to catch the double sunset that tourists go to see, but these girls are doing it ironically, pushing against the boundaries of who they are, where they're from, and where they want to be. They are laughing and singing into the sunset, perfect and alone.

> *The scene shifts to the past, with a similar stage image to that in scene 1. The girls are now fifteen or sixteen.*

ONORA: I feel very ...

WENLOCK: Alive?

EDIE: Yeah, me too.

BELLE: Goodbye sunset and hello darkness.

EDIE: Can we still go to that party, Cowbell?

BELLE: The one at the motel? You wanna go?

ONORA: If it's still happening.

BELLE: Oh, it's always happening.

EDIE: I hear it never ends.

WENLOCK: Will there be anybody we know there?

BELLE: I mean, Jackson'll be there. His friends. We can go
   if you want.

EDIE: I'm in.

ONORA: Wen?

WENLOCK: Sure. Okay.

ONORA: Me too.

> *ALL start to make music and dance by the fire, which
> brings them into the present.*

> *BELLE pours more shots. The action is now drunk,
> playful, light.*

BELLE: And another, here we go!

> *ALL take a shot.*

ONORA: Whoo!

WENLOCK: Yuck.

EDIE: That does not get any better.

WENLOCK: Did you really steal some Munro from the library?

> *BELLE throws books at WENLOCK.*

WENLOCK: I wrote a short story about Alice Munro once. It was
   about a book club, an online book club about Alice Munro
   where the participants were the folks who loved Alice Munro's
   work the most in the entire world. Academics who studied her
   their whole lives and writers and other people who admire her,
   like biologists and archeologists, all there for a book club about
   Alice Munro.

EDIE: You just said "Alice Munro" a lot.

BELLE: Alice Munro. Alice Munro.

WENLOCK: Alice Munro. Alice Munro.

BELLE: Alice.

ONORA: Munro.

WENLOCK: Post Alice.

BELLE: Munro.

EDIE: Okay.

WENLOCK: And we, yes, we, you and me, Belle, were part of the book club, and then we started a podcast where we could talk about our experience of the book club. It was a podcast about a book club.

ONORA: About Alice Munro?

WENLOCK: Yes.

BELLE: There's a farm she describes in this one story. A farm at night where this young girl goes out into the dark to escape her thoughts of murdering her younger sister.

ONORA: Didn't she live on a fox farm outside Wingham somewhere?

BELLE: Yup. Those foxes knew she was out there in the dark, too, I'm sure. Knew she was contemplating death because death was so close to them, so near them, too. The night darkness of the farm is supposed to be a metaphor for something, but I can't figure it out. I hoped it had something to do with adolescence, I love coming of age, about needing to have sex so she wanted to kill her sister, but I think I'm wrong and I just wanted it to be that. Munro, she said something about not getting enough exercise.

WENLOCK: Everyone thinks about killing their sisters. Even people who get enough exercise.

BELLE: Did you?

WENLOCK: This one time I had you in a headlock ...

BELLE: I remember ...

WENLOCK: You were a lot smaller than me, even though you were older.

BELLE: I remember.

WENLOCK: Your hair was yellow then and thin. Much thinner than it is now.

BELLE: I ... remember.

WENLOCK: And there was a moment –

EDIE: Where you wanted to kill her?

WENLOCK: Where I realized I could. I had the power to kill her if I just squeezed a little bit harder. I could pop your head right off.

EDIE makes a popping noise.

WENLOCK: In my story, the podcast turns into a film. We write the film, me and you, but it doesn't matter how great it is because it's post Alice.

ONORA: Munro.

WENLOCK: And that's all the rage. Everyone wants in on the Huron County, Southwestern-Ontario-gothic experience. What's still Munro.

BELLE: Alice.

WENLOCK: What is different and why?

BELLE: It's all the same.

WENLOCK: The film becomes very successful.

EDIE: In the story?

ONORA: In the podcast?

BELLE: In the dream about the film about.

WENLOCK: Post.

ONORA: Alice.

WENLOCK: Munro.

Laughter.

EDIE: I'd like to admit something to you. I don't think I've ever read an Alice Munro story.

BELLE: Never?

EDIE: Maybe, but I don't think so. I don't remember reading one, anyway.

BELLE: I ... well, that's unbelievable really.

EDIE: Is it? I mean, who wants to read something that's supposed to be about you?

ONORA looks at the audience.

ONORA: (*to the audience about the letter, but with a double meaning*) I do. I want to read it.

EDIE: Why?

ONORA: (*also about the letter*) I'm still figuring that out.

WENLOCK: For clues.

ONORA: Clues?

WENLOCK: About how to live. That's why you read, well, I read Alice Munro, anyway. I look for clues in her writing to figure out how we're supposed to live in this bizarre thing called life.

ONORA takes out the letter.

EDIE: What are you doing with that?

ONORA: Not sure yet.

WENLOCK: Take your time.

BELLE: Or don't. Let us in on that fresh new life in there.

ONORA starts to open the letter.

EDIE: Here we go.

WENLOCK: You okay?

ONORA: We'll see.

BELLE: Fresh reasons to get up in the morning.

ONORA: Wait. Can I, uh, can I ask you all a favour?

WENLOCK: Anything.

EDIE: Shoot.

ONORA: When I read it, can you all just stay with me?

BELLE: What do you mean?

ONORA: Can you just be here, just listen, just watch, nothing more, nothing less?

WENLOCK: No talking?

ONORA: Or gasping or sounds, really. Just be?

EDIE: You got it.

WENLOCK: Yeah. Of course.

ONORA: Belle?

BELLE: What? Yeah. Okay.

ONORA: You sure?

BELLE: Yeah. Yes. I'm here.

ONORA: (*reading the letter*) "My girl, I know you. I have known you for a long time. Go to your father and tell him you want to know me too."

    ONORA searches on the page for more, but there is no more.

EDIE: Is that it?

WENLOCK: Edie.

EDIE: Sorry. Sorry, Onora, I was just –

ONORA: It's okay.

> *ONORA discovers her emotions. This can take as long as it needs to.*

ONORA: It's okay.

EDIE: I mean, that wasn't what I was expecting.

ONORA: Me neither. I thought this was an answer, but life's just a little more complicated than that, I guess. Wen?

WENLOCK: Yeah?

ONORA: You with me?

WENLOCK: Right here.

ONORA: You know, I think I know why I like reading stories.

EDIE: Why?

ONORA: What it is for me is that I've measured most things that have happened to me in life against the characters I read in her stories, Munro's and other writers' too. Not measured. That's the wrong word, but they help pull you along. Give you courage for existing.

EDIE: Courage for existing. I like that.

BELLE: I could use some courage for existing these days.

ONORA: Oh Belle –

BELLE: No. No. Please don't look at me like that.

ONORA: Can you please let me at least say I love you?

BELLE: Okay.

EDIE: I also love you.

WENLOCK: We all love you.

BELLE: I know, but I don't need your pity, okay? No dingbat eyes, remember? I know this is going to sound like I made this up, but having a fake leg is something I have always thought was pretty cool. I'm okay with it.

ONORA: Cowbell.

BELLE: This is going to sound not real, so I don't know why I'm even telling you this, but I always kind of knew I was going to lose my leg. I know. I get it, but I swear it's true. At night in bed before I went to sleep when I was probably six or seven, after Mom died and Dad wasn't handling it too well ... I had this ongoing fantasy that I would play out to myself before getting to sleep. I would imagine getting kidnapped out my window. Then I would be taken to this warehouse with beds caged in a row, like an even more fucked-up version of a Victorian orphanage or something where there's a room full of beds with the added horrifying element of a wooden cage around them. Each bed also had a camera attached to it where we knew there was a prince watching us and the general storyline was that this prince would pick one of us from our cage to marry him after watching us for a certain amount of time. I got to know the girl beside me every time and she described her fucked-up life to me and I described my fucked-up life to her. Hers was always even worse than mine, so I always ended up liking her, feeling a need to save her. Sometimes the prince would try one of us out, and yes, that is exactly what it sounds like. Whatever I thought sex was at the time would happen then.

I was usually asleep before the dream or fantasy got much further than that, but sometimes, now this is weird, so brace yourselves. I would cut off my own leg and cut off one of the metal bars (logic doesn't belong here, by the way), I could then slip out between the bars and replace my leg with the metal bar and the metal bar with my leg. I'd teach the girl next to me how to do it, too, switching leg for metal. Both of us running out of there with new metal legs perfectly fused to the rest of our bodies.

Once the metal leg was on, it didn't really feel wrong in any way. It just felt like that was the next step in my escape. So when the doctor told me I've gotta get rid of her, this lady here, I guess I wasn't surprised.

I forgot about these dreams or whatever you want to call them, but about a year ago they started happening again. Jackson started disappearing again for a few nights at a time, and I went back to the warehouse full of girls caged bed-to-bed and fused the metal to my leg to escape.

The sound of revving begins. The time shifts to somewhere between past and present.

WENLOCK: Belle, that night with the sunset when we went to that party at the motel with Jackson and his friends –

BELLE: Wen, I know I brought this up, but I don't know if I can.

WENLOCK: Okay.

ONORA: No. She needs to hear it.

EDIE: We all do. Look, it's not all bad. At the beginning of the party that night, I was feeling good.

ONORA: Yeah. I think we all were.

EDIE: I thought we were fine. I mean, it's not like we hadn't been to a party before.

ONORA: Most people seemed nice.

WENLOCK: Really nice.

ONORA: I didn't know anyone but they all acted like they knew us and not like we were there just to, like, be girls or whatever.

EDIE: I talked to this smoking-hot pilot for a while. He was sweet. I was really self-conscious that day because all of sudden my baby leg hairs were catching the light and they were thicker and longer than I remembered. I was worried everyone was looking at them all day. And when the pilot was talking about how he thought flying was the only thing keeping him alive and off the ground scurrying like a skink in the grass, he really said that ...

ALL: (*in the past as the pilot*) Scurrying like a five-lined skink.

EDIE: He saw me looking at my legs and was right in my head.

ALL: Yeah, women today shave it all off.

EDIE: But he said that I didn't need to.

ALL: It's a sign of being a woman, and what's wrong with that?

EDIE: After we made out a little, he even told me not to waste my time on him because he was engaged and encouraged me to trade my baby five-lined skink life for an airplane someday.

WENLOCK: Jackson seemed interested in my life for the first time.

ONORA: He kept asking all the right questions about Wen's home movies.

ALL: (*in the past as Jackson*) You going to Hollywood?

WENLOCK: No. Hollywood?

ALL: (*in the past as Jackson*) Or no, Europe. That's more your style, right?

WENLOCK: I hadn't even told anybody that's where I wanted to go yet.

ONORA: He said he knew about us, even. Me and Wen.

WENLOCK: And supported our relationship.

ONORA: He was the first person to say that to us. He didn't even whisper it.

ALL: (*speaking as Jackson*) You two give each other light.

WENLOCK: A weird way of putting it.

ONORA: But it felt so nice, too.

WENLOCK: I looked to see if you were there, Belle, if you asked him to say this, maybe, but you weren't there.

> *The sound of revving continues.*

At first I didn't put the two actions together. The money in Jackson's hand and him lifting me onto his friend's bike. It felt impossible.

ONORA: I let you go.

WENLOCK: You couldn't have known. I didn't know. Did you know, Belle?

EDIE: The revving made me turn my head from the pilot. I just watched Wen on the back of that bike fly into the dark.

WENLOCK: It was the bizarre cold politeness of it that I remember most. In the field he didn't say anything, but he neatly folded my clothes and placed them carefully into his bag. I honestly can't be entirely sure about this, but I don't think he touched me. We rode through the fields instead, me clinging to his back, the night coldness numbing me all over. Like it was just about me being completely naked holding on to him that he needed. In my mind I had to prove that I could survive this moment of vulnerability, I could make it through, but who was I proving that to? You, Belle? Where were you?

BELLE: I was young.

WENLOCK: And I was younger.

BELLE: I know. It did feel impossible, somehow. Until I saw you three there with me, and it became all too possible, so that's why I left. Walked home in the dark. Took out a box from the laundry room and pulled all his things off my wall, the jerseys and his name spelled out in photographs above my bed. You might not believe me, but when I got up in the morning they were impossibly back up on the walls and so I thought I must have dreamed it, everything, the sunset, the motel. I know that sounds ... but that was what was true to me then. I realize now Dad, he must have thought he was saving me from myself, meticulously returning Jackson's things to my walls, that's the only logical explanation, allowing him to move in, unboxing more of his life into my teenage bedroom.

EDIE: That wasn't the only time I went to the motel. I asked Jackson to take me there a few more times. It was mostly like before, I met someone nice and talked and made out and it was all fine. And your dad ...

WENLOCK: Go ahead.

EDIE: He was there one night. I started to feel really far away from it all, like my body was in two places at once when he was there, acted like he wasn't surprised to see me, like I belonged there. There was a woman there who looked like Mistie Murray the night my body was in two places. I looked at the other girls there with us. Some faces I recognized, maybe from another life. They looked like staying on a motel bed that night wasn't a surprise to them, like they might not be sure where they would be sleeping the next night, either. Like they might even have other beds to sleep in maybe, safe ones, warm, but they couldn't get back there, not now.

Post Alice: Scene 10 – Post Alice

ALL: Gorgeous five-lined skinks with their blue tails pulled off in the grass.

BELLE: Even though I practised it every night before I went to sleep, I didn't save you. Like the girl in the cage, I should have taught you how to shed your limbs, fuse metal to bone. I practised it every night but when it came to it, I –

WENLOCK: You were young.

ONORA: Belle.

BELLE: Yeah?

ONORA: Belle, you're bleeding again.

The revving sound stops.

SCENE 11
NO TRACE

WENLOCK is in another space and time sort of finishing her pitch, but also kind of talking directly to the audience. BELLE, ONORA, and EDIE join in. A whispering Mistie voice and/or choral singing could be added throughout.

EDIE: (*singing*) In the flames. In the waves. In the sky. In the earth.

ALL: (*singing*) Where do our lost girls go?

WENLOCK: A number of Mistie's friends and other kids she knew said they saw her the days after her disappearance.

ONORA: But police dismissed their sightings.

BELLE: After they had decided it was him, her father.

EDIE: They scoured that lake to find her, but never did.

WENLOCK: Many people believe he had nothing to do with it and she was on the streets in London by then, Toronto maybe, eventually Vancouver.

ALL: (*singing*) Where do our lost girls go?

WENLOCK: And the final image for the film? Yes. I think I have that one too.

EDIE: We started with the sunset.

BELLE: A real bitch.

ONORA: So we leave early in the morning.

WENLOCK: The sunrise sits on the streets.

BELLE: On the windows.

ONORA: On the fields, on the lake.

EDIE: Sunrise on a woman getting into her search-and-rescue aircraft.

BELLE: Sunrise on a woman fitting her newly whittled leg.

ONORA: Sunrise on a woman and her father driving to visit her grandmother.

WENLOCK: After kissing the sunrise in her partner's mouth as she unpacks her life back onto a farm.

EDIE: But if that's too neat an ending for you ...

BELLE: Too final ...

ONORA: Doesn't fit with your version of last night's truth ...

WENLOCK: Maybe it's a sunrise on an empty farm instead. No trace of four wild women screaming into the abyss the night before, no trace of the four children who dared to laugh at something as sacred as a sunset, maybe there's no trace of them at all.

ALL: (*singing*) In the flames. In the waves. In the sky. In the earth. Where do our lost girls go?

The End

POST ALICE IN CONVERSATION

TAYLOR MARIE GRAHAM,
TERRE CHARTRAND, AND
HEATHER MARIE ANNIS

Settler-Canadian playwright and scholar Taylor Marie Graham and non-status Algonquin writer and artist Terre Chartrand discuss their conversation-style cultural exchange and working process on *Post Alice*. Although inspired by four rural women from four short stories by Nobel Prize winning author Alice Munro, the play also references the history of Missing and Murdered Indigenous Women, Girls, and Two-Spirit People in Canada. French, Scottish, and Mi'kmaq actor Heather Marie Annis describes her experience of inhabiting Onora, a character with Haudenosaunee family ancestry in *Post Alice*.

TERRE CHARTRAND is a non-status Algonquin and French Canadian writer, food sovereignty activist, forest guide, seed keeper, artist, and Traditional beader. Terre has been a consultant by various municipal and civic governments in Waterloo Region. Terre currently lives in Nipissing Territory, where she works with the Nipissing Region Curatorial Collective on a variety of projects, including Broken Forests Group.

HEATHER MARIE ANNIS is a Tkarón:to (Toronto) based artist with Mi'kmaq, Scottish, and French heritage. She is an actor, director, playwright, theatrical and therapeutic clown, Co-Artistic Director of U.N.I.T. Productions, and "Morro" of the Dora Award and Canadian Comedy Award winning clown duo Morro and Jasp.

GRAHAM: Summer 2021, my play *Post Alice* was commissioned and produced by the Here For Now Theatre Festival (*HFN*) in Stratford, Ontario. The festival's synopsis of *Post Alice* reads:

> Inspired by four haunting characters from four iconic Alice Munro stories, *Post Alice*, written by Taylor Marie Graham, is a stunning new contemporary play which asks the question: what really happened to Mistie Murray? And what happens to all our missing girls? Come

sit around the fire with four bright and hilarious Huron County women as ghost stories emerge, songs fill the air, family secrets are revealed, and mysteries unravel into those wonderful contradictions which live inside us all.[1]

Post Alice balances my own experiences as a settler-Canadian girl growing up along the shores of Lake Huron, 2013 Nobel laureate Alice Munro's depictions of Huron County, and the problematic legacy of colonial histories embedded within this region.

I grew up in Huron County, Ontario, a place that is often given the toponym Alice Munro Country because of how often Munro depicts the region in her short stories. To demonstrate this regional nickname's popularity, the phrase "Alice Munro Country" is the title for two texts which engage with this area: a short story by Canadian writer Madeleine Thien[2] and a collection of essays on Munro edited by J.R. (*Tim*) Struthers.[3] Munro's biographer Robert Thacker calls Alice Munro Country, "a complexly rendered fictional territory,"[4] and some theorists such as Dennis Duffy have aligned Munro's fiction with problematic settler-colonial Canadian narratives which, among other injustices, erase Indigenous Peoples, cultures, and histories from the region.

In *Post Alice*, along with the inclusion of fictional characters inspired by Munro's protagonists, I also weave in a true story. In 1995, when I was nine years old, a Huron County teenager named Mistie Murray went missing. Adopted at an early age, Mistie's biological mother was Mi'kmaq, which connects Mistie's story to the violent and deeply difficult history of Missing and Murdered Indigenous Women, Girls, and Two-Spirit People (*MMIWG2S*) in the land now referred to as Canada. According to the 2019 Final Report of the National Inquiry into MMIWG2S, because of colonial injustices that still exist in Canadian society today, "Indigenous women and girls are twelve times more likely to be murdered or missing than any other women in Canada."[5] Among the many important calls to action, The Final Report calls on all Canadians to:

Decolonize by learning the true history of Canada and Indigenous history in [their] local area. Learn about and celebrate Indigenous Peoples' history, cultures, pride, and diversity, acknowledging the land [they] live on and its importance to local Indigenous communities, both historically and today.[6]

In an effort to support this call to education of Indigenous histories from the Final Report on MMIWG2S, I invited non-status[7] Algonquin and French Canadian artist Terre Chartrand to work with me on *Post Alice*. Chartrand led me through a series of oral storytelling exchanges. Our work focused on the development of the fictional character Onora, who has Haudenosaunee family on her father's side, and the inclusion of Mistie Murray's true story in the play. The critical reception of the play was quite positive, often remarking on the content developed from our working sessions, although it should be noted that none of the reviewers were Indigenous. Joe Szekeres described the play as "Powerful, powerful, and courageous."[8] Lynn Slotkin called the play "arresting" and specifically mentions the play's link to MMIWG2S as "deepening the play, giving it resonance."[9] Christopher Hoile was particularly positive, giving *Post Alice* a five-star review and calling it "one of the best new Canadian plays I've seen in a long time."[10]

Working in this way with Chartrand was a unique, humbling, and extremely rewarding experience for me as a settler-Canadian playwright. After the play finished its premiere run, I asked if we could sit down to debrief our working process together. I was curious to learn about Chartrand's experience of our working sessions. Did she find it as positive an exchange as I did? Was there more I could have done to ensure it was a safe and reciprocal experience for her?

Chartrand met with me over a series of online calls, and we began unpacking our oral story-exchange work on *Post Alice*. Soon after starting, we realized that we also wanted to learn from Heather Marie Annis, the French, Scottish, and Mi'kmaq actor who played the character of Onora in *Post Alice*, so I invited her to share her experience of working on the project as well. Chartrand and I became aware that this kind of debrief dialogue, one that reached across settler-Indigenous divides, was potentially useful for other artists and academics who were interested in working in a similar way. According to writer and educator Cynthia Cohen, "artistic processes can create opportunities for interaction among factions alienated from each other and facilitate opportunities for them to imagine together and co-create a better future."[11] Our discussion could provide one example of a creation methodology that other settler and Indigenous theatre-makers could employ to work across, illuminate, and disrupt existing divides.

What follows is an edited discussion between me and Chartrand from a series of online calls. Included within our discussion is a reflection from Heather Marie Annis from another online call. My hope is that by sharing this post-mortem, other artists, scholars, and the wider public can learn from our successes, failures, and all the complex spaces in between while working on *Post Alice*.

• • •

GRAHAM: Terre, in 2021 we worked together in a way that I haven't experienced before. When I write a play, I usually sit in a dark room on my own all day until it's done.

CHARTRAND: (*laughs*)

GRAHAM: I knew this process wasn't going to work for me this time. When you came onto the project, you taught me so much throughout our sessions together. I want to thank you again for patiently helping me as I developed *Post Alice*. It was incredibly rewarding working with you.

CHARTRAND: You're very welcome. I'm so happy to hear that you had such a positive experience. I really enjoyed working with you, too. I was thinking that before we start talking about our story-sharing process together, it might be useful to go back to some of your first impulses as a playwright on this project. Can you maybe talk a little bit more about why it was necessary or important to you to explore decolonial themes in *Post Alice*?

GRAHAM: Sure. Of course. It's a number of reasons coming together at once. Like life, the writing process for me is often complicated; and I like to lean into the complications because that's often where the important topics live.

CHARTRAND: I like that.

GRAHAM: At first, I thought this play would be mostly inspired by four female settler protagonists from my favourite Alice Munro stories and my experience of growing up as a girl in Alice Munro Country in Huron County. But I also wanted to include the beautiful and complex rural women of the region who have often been erased from literature, media, and public consciousness due to misogyny and colonialism in Canadian society.

CHARTRAND: That's a big responsibility.

GRAHAM: Absolutely. And I remember feeling that weight of that responsibility at the time, too, not sure if I should even attempt to write this play at all.

CHARTRAND: I can understand that.

GRAHAM: I was also grappling with my own white privilege at the time, recognizing that there was room to interrogate the way I was working, how I could open up my process to decolonial methods.

CHARTRAND: Where was this all coming from, do you think?

GRAHAM: Just before and while I was writing *Post Alice*, I was also completing doctoral exams in post-colonial literatures and theatre from Nigeria, Kenya, South Africa, Ireland, and Canada. I spent a year of intense reading and research of authors such as Frantz Fanon, Wole Soyinka, Tom Murphy, Brian Friel, Keith Barker, Yvette Nolan, and Drew Hayden Taylor, just to name a few. I was steeped in theory, plays, and novels examining decolonial themes at the time. Each region has a specific history and culture that made its mark on me.

As a person who has always enjoyed having both an academic and creative-writing life, my academic work has always impacted my creative writing and vice versa. They usually feel in conversation with each other. I felt the need to do more than write academically about what I was reading at the time. I felt compelled to apply this learning and unlearning to my creative work as well.

My first thought was to write about white ambiguity, which I felt more comfortable inhabiting, and could understand from my own experience. So this is what I started to do. Within the play there are settler characters who realize their ignorance of MMIWG2S. But as

I was writing this, I didn't feel like I was going far enough, digging deep enough.

CHARTRAND: Is that where Mistie came in?

GRAHAM: It is. As you know, when I was a young girl in grade school, Mistie Murray went missing from the high school up the road where my mother taught. Mistie's mother was also a kindergarten teacher at my school at the time, and this event shook the whole community for years afterwards. Poor Mistie was never found.

At the time she went missing and for many years afterwards, I didn't know Mistie's biological mother was Mi'kmaq. While Mistie grew up in a settler adopted family for most of her short life, her biological mother's identity was an important part of her story that I didn't hear about growing up. It's only been in the last ten years or so that MMIWG2S has become a national news item, not hidden away, erased out of colonial shame. But of course, many Indigenous people have been speaking out about this violence for years. I was regrettably one of those Canadians tuned out of their voices until more recently.

CHARTRAND: Like so many.

GRAHAM: I was determined that my play not add to the historical violence and erasure of Indigenous women in literature in Canada. But I wasn't sure if I should explore this story, though, and am still grappling with this question, to be honest, because it's not my story to tell in many ways. I was affected by Mistie's story, but it did not happen to me directly. What I started to write about were the women and girls affected by Mistie's story. Again, I felt that this didn't go far enough, though. I felt compelled to do more, have one of the women in the story learn about her own Indigenous ancestry, but I am not Indigenous.

CHARTRAND: No. You are not.

GRAHAM: That's when I invited you to meet with me, Terre. We met in a playwright unit in 2017. I certainly felt a kinship with you throughout that time, as well as a deep admiration for your work. That's why I reached out to you specifically to see if you would be willing to work with me.

I'm curious though, and please feel free to be honest with me, what was your first reaction when I reached out to you about this project?

CHARTRAND: Well, because it was you, I had a high degree of trust already for your writing and the process, but I also hesitated because it cuts so close, you know?

GRAHAM: Absolutely.

CHARTRAND: You know, there's a difference between being naked and nude. Nakedness is hard and harsh. Nude, you could be on display, but it's more of a reverential concept. So in that first conversation I was wondering: okay, in this process, am I going to be naked or nude? Because that depends on our interactions.

Our conversation turned into something that became a deeper, intimate space right away. A space of liminality. We entered a ceremonial space together. I felt compelled to share personal stories with you because that trust was there. I trusted that what I was offering you was just between you and me. That you would let this inspire you to write a fictional story and not steal the exact stories I was telling you.

GRAHAM: I felt that immediately, this sense of you really being that vulnerable with me and the immense responsibility that came with that. I was also very aware of the fact I might be doing everything wrong and so I was trying to be as open to being guided by you throughout this process as possible.

CHARTRAND: I think we did really well. I think there was a mutuality in the work. At first I remember thinking, I'm not quite sure what she's hoping this will be. I think you weren't exactly sure what you were hoping for either?

GRAHAM: I wasn't. All I knew intuitively and from my academic research, too, I suppose, was that I needed to listen and be open like I would in any creative exchange, but there was an added layer of vulnerability for both of us, I think.

CHARTRAND: I think that's because we were diving into a cross-cultural exchange that isn't frequent, a coming back to story. There's always a person who tells and a person who receives and a between those two places. And the person who's telling is encoding it to try to tell it in the best way for that person who's receiving it.

For me there's a real responsibility around story, very profound. A lot of our most cherished stories are still ones that are within the space of oral tradition. We all love stories. Children love hearing stories about their younger selves, right?

When you're ten, you might love hearing about what happened when you were five, for example. I love hearing my mother's stories about her younger self. I love hearing my sister's stories about how she remembers a moment from our childhood, especially if I don't remember it that way at all.

GRAHAM: Beautiful. Yes.

CHARTRAND: Indigenous stories are all like that because they're all related to ourselves and our people. They are a cherished piece of identity within that container.

Can I ask what you were experiencing as I was telling you these stories?

GRAHAM: I remember trying to really hear what you were telling me, trying my best not to project my own expectations on what you were telling me, trying my best not to lead you, interrupt, or change the flow of conversation.

CHARTRAND: I sensed that.

GRAHAM: I think a lot of writers probably feel this way, this sense of being able to be open and listening to the world, but there's a difference between being open and listening and fully understanding, fully being able to.

Without sharing the exact stories you told me because that was just for us, I can perhaps also share the intense feeling I had while you were sharing and afterwards?

CHARTRAND: Please go ahead.

GRAHAM: What I was struck with was facing the complexities of a full human with a complex life. The fullness of your existence is what stuck with me the most in that process and the beautiful paradoxes of living a full existence. Your story's richness stood out. It required recognition of depth and complexity within your journey.

CHARTRAND: That's wonderful to hear. It means a lot to me to know that was the effect for you of the process.

GRAHAM: Thinking more about oral storytelling for a minute, I love hearing you talk about what it means to you. Do you mind talking a little bit about where you see the differences between oral and written transmission?

CHARTRAND: One aspect to oral transmission that sometimes surprises people who are unfamiliar with its process in Indigenous cultures is the correctness.

GRAHAM: What do you mean by correctness?

CHARTRAND: There's a learning process that takes time. You must repeat back to your teacher several times. For example, when I was recently taught a song by a friend, we first spent an hour learning the song. Then my friend who gave me the song called me back three days later and said, "Okay. I wanna hear it again." I sang it to her and she corrected the bits I got wrong. A week later, this happened again. She heard me sing the song and she gave me feedback. A few months later she heard it again and she said, "Yes. You got it." It's a process of verification, one that exists with a lot of stories that I don't think happens necessarily when we sit down and write.

GRAHAM: Thank you for sharing that, Terre.

CHARTRAND: Oral storytelling is powerful. It's one thing to see in text that the Indian Act took away Indigenous population's rights, but a story about a specific person's experience allows room for empathy and a more complex understanding of this experience.

But there's a big gap between experiencing and witnessing. Without a close and lived experience, it's proximity, but proximity to Indigeneity doesn't make Indigeneity.

GRAHAM: Right. Yes.

CHARTRAND: Which ended up trickling into the character you created. Onora, your fictional character, is learning about her father's family, who is Haudenosaunee. It was important for me to share with you that many Indigenous family lines are matrilineal and there's a lot of difficult history of who gets to claim status in Canada, who has had it ripped away, etc. I know you didn't want your play to be about this exactly, but I thought it was vital that Onora be in that liminal space, that space of learning, witnessing.

GRAHAM: That distinction between experiencing and witnessing for Onora was so important. The character was just starting to learn about her father's family history, about what was hidden from her, from society, and her own family. I originally wrote Onora as if she didn't have any knowledge of her father's heritage whatsoever growing up, but after speaking to you that didn't seem quite right. You led me to a place where Onora would always have a heightened sense that an aspect of her family's history hadn't been fully revealed to her growing up. She had a desire to research and understand more, but was continually coming up against a lot of barriers, coming up short in her search, until now.

CHARTRAND: I'm so glad I could help you find that journey in the story. You also ended up giving Onora direct address monologues, which her friends couldn't hear.

GRAHAM: This was also directly inspired by our working together, Terre, me listening to your stories.

CHARTRAND: I thought it was very effective. To me Onora's monologues did two things: it gave her an interior life that her friends didn't have access to and it also implicated the audience in Onora's journey.

GRAHAM: Thank you. It makes me really happy to hear you say that. I should mention, too, that throughout the rehearsal process, Heather Marie Annis, the incredibly talented actor who played Onora, provided feedback on these monologues as well, helping to shape them further. I really lucked out with the whole creative team. The wonderfully sensitive director Fiona Mongillo, Heather, and the other phenomenal actors Aubree Erickson, Ellen Denny, and Siobhan O'Malley, made it a priority to give each character a lot of depth. They discovered and explored the complicated history that exists for each character individually and as a collective.

Because the play was only sixty minutes and I was writing about four complex women, I was also acutely aware I could not explore Onora's entire life fully in her time on stage. I felt I could give the audience one small moment in Onora's journey of discovery, a small opening. The play itself takes place over the course of one night outside at a fire with old friends, so small moments of reveal that have an enormous personal impact and propel the characters forward felt like the best way to go all around.

Onora's reveal was just a first step, a first toe in the water of learning a little about her own family. This also meant that she was still in the learning phase.

CHARTRAND: This might be a good place to bring Heather's reflection into the conversation.

GRAHAM: That's a great idea.

CHARTRAND: We can pick up our chat after sharing Heather's insights into her experience of the process.

ANNIS: When my agent told me about the role of Onora from *Post Alice* my first response was, I don't know if I'm right for the part, if I should be the person auditioning for this role. If a part is listed for an Indigenous actor, I don't submit for it. I am a white person, and I don't want to accept roles that belong to other people. When I was asked to audition, I had a bit of an internal conflict, to be honest.

Then I read the play and discovered that this character is learning about their past and their Indigenous heritage within the story, which is also true for me. This character also passes as white. This made me feel like it was a role I could consider, and after speaking with the director Fiona Mongillo, I came to a place where I felt more comfortable with it.

I don't ever want to put myself in a position where I'm speaking on behalf of Indigenous people or as an expert on Indigeneity.

I am part Indigenous, Mi'kmaq, but also have mixed settler ancestry. My grandparents had to pretend not to be Indigenous, and their culture was taken away from me and the rest of our family because of this. Although my grandfather did practice Traditional ways of knowledge until he passed away, I learned about most of it as I became an adult.

There's so much conversation right now about who gets to speak to which identities. And I think that when people get in trouble, it's when they're not honest and pretend to be an authority on a culture that is not their own. When they're representing other peoples' voices without care, reflection, and understanding.

When I got into rehearsals, I was trying to find my way into the character, find how I relate to Onora, as you do with any character. I found there were several links to my own history and family which helped situate me. As I learned more about Onora, I discovered a lot was purposefully left off the page, as inspired by Munro's writing style. Onora's search for her own identity and personal experience of Indigenous missing women was very present, but sometimes between the lines. There was a part of me that wanted to advocate for the play to be more about Onora's story and focus more on these elements, but I wondered if that was a selfish actor request or being an advocate for an important story. With the horrific discoveries of burial sites of Indigenous children at residential schools in the news at the time of rehearsals, I had a conversation with Taylor, inviting her to bring more of Onora's role onstage throughout the play. This led to more of this depth and layers being added to Onora's internal monologues.

Fiona had such a beautiful, collaborative directing style for this production. If someone had an idea, she would hear it. In this spirit, we collectively built a visual homage to The REDress Project, "an aesthetic response to the more than 1,000 missing and murdered Aboriginal Women in Canada," by Anishinaabe and Finnish artist Jaime Black.[12] Throughout Taylor's song about lost girls (*which takes place midway through the play*), Onora held and hung up a piece of red cloth which flowed gently in the wind, visible throughout the rest of the show. This moment was something I struggled with, though, and still do. With it we are suggesting links to Indigenous women, but the show doesn't fully dig into the topic's full complexity. We're letting those stories into the space, and I think we could do more to honour them. This is of course difficult to fully do in an hour-long play with four complex characters all deserving of stage time, but I do think there's room to explore more possibilities.

After so many great chats with Taylor, and with the goal of another production soon, I'm excited to continue asking questions and working together to find out how we might do more to honour these important Indigenous women, girls, and two-spirit people in *Post Alice*.

• • •

CHARTRAND: I'm so grateful to Heather for sharing her experience.

GRAHAM: Me too! She offers a lot to think through, especially concerning her thought process before auditioning and the visual aspects of the production which honour MMIWG2S. All theatre is collaborative, and this team's investment in finding a visual vocabulary for *Post Alice* which complemented the themes in the script was exemplary, with room to grow in potential future productions. Heather's such a generous collaborator, and I'm so thankful to her for her contributions and for being open to script edits based on her feedback throughout rehearsals – including only days before opening night! What a gift to have an actor so committed to making a play's premiere production as strong as it can be.

CHARTRAND: That's so important for a new play. One part from Heather's reflection that stands out to me is when she mentions that Onora is coded as white in society. This is another reason I felt I could help you with this story. I have pale skin and light eyes. If you wanted to write about the racialized experience of an Indigenous person, I would have told you that you needed someone who has a closer phenotype, someone who has brown skin. I can tell you just walking around with brown-skin friends, partners, relatives, I don't experience what they do and it's daily and it's nonstop mitigation. I can't assume what my brown-skin grandmother went through in the thirties and forties as a woman.

When we were talking throughout our working sessions, Taylor, I felt it was important to share stories addressing the non-existence of pan-Indigeneity, too. It's the same with whiteness. Again, it's one of those points that's easy to say, but sharing a story allows a deeper understanding.

GRAHAM: I'm curious what you specifically think about theatre then, Terre? Where does it sit for you in the oral vs. written scale?

CHARTRAND: Once something is published, there's a sense of finality. It can't change in the way that it can when it's still in the oral tradition. I don't have a problem with publishing work, exactly, but before a play is published it can live in a liminal space. Theatre is liminal. Liminality is a space in-between and before. So it's a ceremonial space.

GRAHAM: There's something else related to this topic that I wanted to ask you about. What do you make of this play not being verbatim theatre? You shared your stories with me, but I let this inspire a fictional character rather than using your exact words. Artists such as Nikki Owusu Yeboah provide arguments for processes rooted in verbatim theatre to honour the "responsibility [of] scholars, activists, and artists invested in the work of oral-history performance in the age of trauma culture."[13] I wondered about this as I was writing *Post Alice* and built this question into the story itself. One of the settler characters who is a filmmaker grapples with questions of documentary vs. fiction in telling Mistie Murray's story in a new film. Mistie's story is a real story in the midst of a fictional narrative. There's the argument that fictionalizing stories about Indigenous women is another form of erasure, and some artists and scholars believe that the way to actively work against this is to use the exact text from Indigenous artists like yourself rather than fictionalizing the content through a white-settler lens.

CHARTRAND: There's a lot to unpack here, and I think there's a lot of reasons why verbatim theatre may be the right choice for some productions. Thinking specifically about our process, I liked the separation between my exact lived experience and Onora's fictional one. I honestly was more comfortable, because we were creating someone who could embody parts of my story who wasn't just an analogue for me.

I deeply appreciated your translation of some of my experiences into the character of Onora. I have done translations with people before, because I speak two languages. It requires a proper writing of the text in English and then a real go-over to make sure the translation maintains meaning. I felt like our process reflected this.

Was my own story lost in this fictional play? No. It exists in another way here. Do I feel as though I am made invisible within the context of lending a story? No. I don't.

I think it would require absolute Indigenous authorship to write an Indigenous story in its entirety, but that's not what you were doing. I think the fictionalization allowed us the room in the space between us. This process in many ways was about trying to figure out how Indigenous characters, issues, and stories exist within white stories and fictions today.

GRAHAM: You may have sensed this next question coming. I wanted to talk to you about authorship, Terre. Throughout the process of writing *Post Alice,* I asked you about co-authorship. I offered it to you repeatedly because I wanted to make sure our process was reciprocal, but you've always said you were more comfortable in a consultant or advisory role. Looking back on this now, do you feel this is the right credit for your work on this play? Just to clarify for those reading, you were paid for your work with me at an hourly rate by the HFN.

CHARTRAND: I still don't regret my choice because of where I was at the moment of working with you and my own feelings of precarity. I was happy to stick with an acknowledgement that made me feel safe at the time. There's a lot to think through on the topic of authorship. I was sharing stories, but you were writing, creating the play. I still think cultural consultant was the right title for me on this project and the payment was suitable for the work I was doing.

GRAHAM: Just so you know, if I do ever have an opportunity to publish *Post Alice,* I'll ask you about authorship again.[14] I am very aware of the exploitative histories of extraction, both physical and cultural, that exist within colonial frameworks. Canadian theatre is complicit in this history, too. Alan Filewod, for example, writes about this in his article "Playing on Indigenous Land: Settlers, Immigrants, and Theatre in Fictive Canada."[15] Throughout the process of writing the play, I was very worried that I was participating in another form of cultural extraction.

CHARTRAND: Yeah. I know. I could feel that. I think part of the reason why we had such, such a productive process – I hate that word, but, like, we really did produce a lot of story-knowledge exchange – the reason we were so productive was because you were already thinking in these ways. You already acknowledged this history and were conscious of it throughout the process. I don't think we even spoke it out loud to each other, but it was apparent in how you were working, the kindness you showed me throughout the process, making sure I was cared for in the way I told you I needed. I think you have an excellent barometer for those things already, and I think you know that it was probably in part your academic learning. But I also think you have that just as a human in general.

GRAHAM: Thank you so much. I know I learned a lot throughout this process from both you and Heather. It can be humbling to be a position of learning, of accepting what you can't fully understand, of trying to recognize your own limitations as a creator. It asked me to re-examine my previous methodologies in order to embrace something new. I like this quote from Cynthia Cohen which explains this concept quite well:

> Commitment to robust inclusion is far easier to embrace in theory than to execute in practice. When working to strengthen understanding and relationships between those identified as victims and as perpetrators, people generally need to "unlearn" parts of what they assume to be true about their own and each other's communities.[16]

I've also been thinking that our discussion reminds me of a similar exchange which exists between settler-Canadian artist Linda Griffiths and Métis author Maria Campbell at the beginning of their 1996 play *The Book of Jessica.* I have read this frank and probing dialogue many times, and each reading has provided me with new avenues in which to examine my own white privilege as a settler artist in Canadian society and question the colonial frameworks that reinforce deep-seeded and racist ideologies. This text was an important education to me as a settler-Canadian. It reveals "the ways in which public spaces and national discourses privilege certain bodies and contribute to the ongoing oppression of others."[17] Campbell and Griffiths do this by not only highlighting the successes, but also the difficulties throughout the journey of the play's creation. I hope our discussion can be as useful to others as Campbell and Griffiths's was to me.

To outline our process a little more concretely for those who want

Post Alice in Conversation

to try it out, I'd say the first step was establishing trust between us. Do you agree?

CHARTRAND: Yes. We worked together for about six months getting to know one another as part of the playwrights unit. This might not be realistic for everyone, but establishing trust is key. And then you approached me, making the offer for *Post Alice* as clear as you could with parameters for payment and timelines.

GRAHAM: And I deferred to your knowledge to suggest how we should work together. I followed your lead concerning schedule and work methods.

CHARTRAND: The rest was story exchange. You outlined aspects of the play you wanted to include, and I shared stories that I thought might be useful to your play's development.

GRAHAM: You also read over drafts and attended workshop readings. You provided feedback and shared more oral stories to think through.

The process felt more organic than what we just described, more layered, as hopefully the rest of our discussion demonstrates, but those were the general steps. For a last word, Terre, I'm curious what do you hope people take away from this discussion?

CHARTRAND: I hope people try this process. In the discussions around appropriation, I hope many people approach writing characters from marginalized populations with more care. Creating theatre that touches on other cultures, and especially marginalized people, is possible. The reality is that we live in societies of plurality and so texts must contain diversity. But it must be done through empowered collaboration. This is one method to try.

This appendix is derived in part from an article published in *Research in Drama Education: The Journal of Applied Theatre and Performance*, May 2023, copyright Taylor & Francis, available online at www.tandfonline.com/10.1080/13569783.2023.2168187.

ENDNOTES

1   Here For Now Theatre, "Past Productions, 2021 Season," Here For Now Theatre (website), 2021, www.herefornowtheatre.com/past-productions-2021.

2   Madeleine Thien, "10^80 Pieces," *Globe and Mail*, December 23, 2016, www.theglobeandmail.com/arts/books-and-media/1080-pieces-a-new-short-story-from-madeleinethien/article33422073/.

3   J.R. (Tim) Struthers, ed., *Alice Munro Country: Essays on Her Works I*, (Montréal: Guernica Editions, 2020).

4   Robert Thacker, "Alice Munro's Ontario," in *Reading Alice Munro, 1973–2013* (Calgary: University of Calgary Press, 2016), 203.

5   National Inquiry into Missing and Murdered Indigenous Women and Girls, *Reclaiming Power and Place: The Final Report of the National Inquiry into Missing and Murdered Indigenous Women and Girls*, vol. 1a ([Gatineau]: National Inquiry into Missing and Murdered Indigenous Women and Girls, 2019), 55.

6   National Inquiry into Missing and Murdered Indigenous Women and Girls, *Reclaiming Power and Place: The Final Report of the National Inquiry into Missing and Murdered Indigenous Women and Girls*, vol. 1b ([Gatineau]: National Inquiry into Missing and Murdered Indigenous Women and Girls, 2019), 199.

7   "'Non-Status Indians' commonly refers to people who identify themselves as Indians but who are not entitled to registration on the Indian Register pursuant to the Indian Act. Some may however be members of a First Nation band," Government of Canada, "Non-Status Indians," Canada.ca., last modified September 3, 2012, www.rcaanc-cirnac.gc.ca/eng/1100100014433/1535469348029.

8   Joe Szekeres, "Review: 'Post Alice' as part of Stratford Ontario's HERE FOR NOW NEW WORKS Festival," OnStage Blog, July 28, 2021, www.onstageblog.com/reviews/2021/7/28/review-post-alice-as-part-of-stratford-ontarios-here-for-now-new-works-festival.

9   Lynn Slotkin, "Reviews: Janet and Louise and Post Alice, at the Here for Now Theatre, 2021 New Works Festival, Stratford, Ont," The Slotkin Letter (website), July 28, 2021, slotkinletter.com/2021/07/reviews-janet-and-louise-and-post-alice-at-the-here-for-now-theatre-2021-new-works-festival.

10   Christopher Hoile, "Stage Door Review 2021: Post Alice," Stage Door (website), August 6, 2021, www.stage-door.com/3/2021-Reviews/Entries/2021/8/post-alice-1.html.

11   Cynthia E. Cohen, "Reimagining Transitional Justice," *International Journal of Transitional Justice* 14, 1 (March 2020): 2–3.

12   Jaime Black, "The REDress Project," Jamie Black (website), 2020, www.jaime-blackartist.com/exhibitions/.

13   Nikki Owusu Yeboah, "'I Know How It Is When Nobody Sees You': Oral-History

Performance Methods for Staging Trauma," *Text and Performance Quarterly* 40, 2 (2020): 149.

14   When Taylor learned that Talonbooks was going to publish *Post Alice*, she reached out to Terre again to ask about authorship. Terre reiterated that she felt the role of cultural consultant was most suitable for her work on this project.

15   Alan Filewod, "Playing on Indigenous Land: Settlers, Immigrants, and Theatre in Fictive Canada," in *Theatre and (Im)migration: New Essays on Canadian Theatre,* ed. Yana Meerzon, (Toronto: Playwrights Canada Press, 2019), 27.

16   Cohen, 4.

17   Dylan Robinson and Keavy Martin, "The Body is a Resonant Chamber," in *Arts of Engagement: Taking Aesthetic Action In and Beyond the Truth and Reconciliation Commission of Canada, eds. Dylan Robinson and Keavy Martin* (Waterloo, ON: Wilfrid Laurier University Press, 2016), 3.

WORKS CITED

Black, Jaime. "The REDress Project." Jamie Black (website). 2020. www.jaimeblack-artist.com/exhibitions/.

Cohen, Cynthia E. "Reimagining Transitional Justice." *International Journal of Transitional Justice* 14, no. 1 (March 2020): 1–13. doi.org/10.1093/ijtj/ijaa001.

Filewod, Alan. "Playing on Indigenous Land: Settlers, Immigrants, and Theatre in Fictive Canada." In *Theatre and (Im)migration: New Essays on Canadian Theatre,* edited by Yana Meerzon, 27–55. Toronto: Playwrights Canada Press, 2019.

Government of Canada. "Non-Status Indians." Canada.ca. Last modified September 3, 2012. www.rcaanc-cirnac.gc.ca/eng/1100100014433/1535469348029.

Here For Now Theatre. "Past Productions, 2021 Season." Here For Now Theatre (website). 2021. www.herefornowtheatre.com/past-productions-2021.

Hoile, Christopher. "Stage Door Review 2021: Post Alice." Stage Door (website). August 6, 2021. www.stage-door.com/3/2021-Reviews/Entries/2021/8/post-alice-1.html.

National Inquiry into Missing and Murdered Indigenous Women and Girls. *Reclaiming Power and Place: The Final Report of the National Inquiry into Missing and Murdered Indigenous Women and Girls.* 2 Vols. [Gatineau]: National Inquiry into Missing and Murdered Indigenous Women and Girls, 2019. www.mmiwg-ffada.ca/final-report/.

Robinson, Dylan, and Keavy Martin, editors. *Arts of Engagement: Taking Aesthetic Action In and Beyond the Truth and Reconciliation Commission of Canada.* Waterloo, ON: Wilfrid Laurier University Press, 2016.

Slotkin, Lynn. "Reviews: Janet and Louise and Post Alice, at the Here for Now Theatre, 2021 New Works Festival, Stratford, Ont." The Slotkin Letter (website). July 28, 2021. slotkinletter.com/2021/07/reviews-janet-and-louise-and-post-alice-at-the-here-for-now-theatre-2021-new-works-festival.

Struthers, J.R. (Tim). "A Bibliographical Tour of Alice Munro Country." In *Alice Munro Country: Essays on Her Works I,* edited by J.R. (Tim) Struthers. Montréal: Guernica Editions, 2020.

Szekeres, Joe. "Review: 'Post Alice' as part of Stratford Ontario's HERE FOR NOW NEW WORKS Festival." OnStage Blog. July 28, 2021. www.onstageblog.com/reviews/2021/7/28/review-post-alice-as-part-of-stratford-ontarios-here-for-now-new-works-festival?rq=post%20alice.

Thacker, Robert. "Alice Munro's Ontario." In *Reading Alice Munro, 1973–2013* (Calgary: University of Calgary Press, 2016).

Yeboah, Nikki Owusu. "'I Know How It Is When Nobody Sees You': Oral-History Performance Methods for Staging Trauma." *Text and Performance Quarterly* 40, no. 2 (2020): 131–151. doi.org/10.1080/10462937.2020.1788133.

A NOTE ON PERMISSIONS

Thank you to Anne Murray for permission to include her adopted daughter Mistie Murray's story in *Post Alice* and to Jocelyn Laberge for permission to include her father Normand J. Laberge's obituary in *Cottage Radio*.

ACKNOWLEDGMENTS

A great many people helped me with the three plays found in this book.

First and foremost, I am exceedingly grateful to the wonderful Judith Thompson, who has been the most supportive and incredible mentor a playwright could ever ask for.

I would like to sincerely thank the following fantastic people who assisted the development of one or more of these works in various ways: Abby Weisbrot, Alan Filewod, Alex Albert, Amanda Pereira, Andrea Romaldi, Andrew Kaufman, Andrew Knudson, Anna Fontaine and family, Anne Murray and family, Aubree Erickson, Barb Sebben and family, Betty Thomasson and Bruce Thomasson, Bruna Piccinin and Mario Piccinin, Caitlyn Fysh, Candace Hill, Catherine Bush, Cass Van Wyck, Cathy Cove, Cathy Ryan and Scott Ryan, Christine Groom, Daniel Cristofori, Dan Graham, Danica Fogarty, Dave Martin, Deanna Kruger, Dionne Brand, Eleanor Graham and Hugh Graham, Elizabeth Cooper, Ellen Denny, Emma Atkin, Emma Haase, Emily Jenkins, Ermina Pérez, Fiona Mongillo, Flannery Clare Muise, Gabrielle D'Angelo, Ger Gilmore, Gerry Graham, Gil Garratt, Gregor Campbell, Heather Marie Annis, Ian Lupton, Jan and Jon Jamula, Jeanette Dagger, Jean-Phillipe Allanby, Jenna Meyers and Curtis Meyers, Jenna Turk, Jessica MacDonald, Jessica Ryan, Jill Harper, Jocelyn Cockburn, Jonas Bonnetta, Joshua Browne, J.R. (Tim) Struthers, Judith Rukakoff, Julia Haist, Julia Pileggi, Kalina Janik, Kate Johnston, Katie Thomasson, Katy Graham and Tom Graham, Kara Graham, Kayla Whelan, Kelly McIntosh, Lara Mrkoci, Lauren Wolanski, Lindsay Woods, Lindy Linfield, Lisa Alves, Lisa Jamula, Lisa O'Connell, Liz Howard, Lynette Blanchard, Madeline Leon, Maggie Graham and family, Mark Payne, Mary Cull, Marysia Bucholc, Matt Drappel, Maurissa Meyers, Michael Winter, Mike Piccinin and family, Molly Graham, Molly Mikola, Monique Lund, the Murdock Family, Nicole Smith, Paul Barrett, the people of Goderich, Robert Thacker, Ronnie Mastronardi, Roselyn Kelada-Sedra, Ryan Porter, Sasha Singer-Wilson, Sarah Roger, Sabrina Spence, Sebastian Biasucci, Simon Rossiter, Siobhan O'Malley, Steph Berntson, Susan Loube, Susan Meyers and Bill Meyers, Tara Cooper, Tiana Asperjan, Tim Graham, Terre Chartrand, Terry Piccinin, Toni Hanson, Tony Piccinin and Mary Piccinin, Tracy Ware, Tyler Boucher,

Vladimir Jon Cubrt, Wanda Keith, Wendy Ewert, Yolanda Ferrato, and many more.

My appreciation also extends to the following organizations who supported the works in this collection in various capacities: 4th Line Theatre, the Alice Munro Book Club, the Alice Munro Festival of the Short Story, Alumnae Theatre, Artscape Youngplace, the Blyth Festival Theatre, the Bruce Hotel, the Goderich BIA, the Livery Theatre in Goderich, Here For Now Theatre, the Huron County Museum, the Kitchener-Waterloo Art Gallery, Matchstick Theatre Company, the Ontario Arts Council, Pat the Dog Theatre Creation, the Playwrights Guild of Canada, the PLEDGE Project, Port Albert Productions, the University of Guelph School of English and Theatre Studies, St. Mary's Catholic Elementary School, Theatre Gargantua, the Toronto Fringe Festival, the Arts Awards of Waterloo Region, and the Women's Work Festival.

A very special thank you to Kevin Williams, Catriona Strang, and the rest of the team at Talonbooks for putting together this beautiful book.

Acknowledgments

Taylor Marie Graham is an award-winning playwright, librettist, director, Canadian theatre researcher, and educator. She lives and works
in Cambridge, Ontario, on Treaty 3 Territory. Her Ph.D. research is
focused on the Blyth Festival Theatre found in Huron County and on
theatre's relationship to questions of nationhood, identity, decoloniza-
tion, community engagement, and legacy. *Cottage Radio and Other
Plays* is her first published collection of plays.